DIAMOND HILL

"*Diamond Hill* is an excellent and fast read for those who want an honest depiction of life for a majority of Hong Kong denizens in the 1950s–60s."
— *The Correspondent*

"The harsh but colourful world in which Feng grew up is no more. Once upon a time, Hong Kong was one big squatter village that transformed into a manufacturing Mecca and then again into the financial centre that it is today ... his memoir invokes a toughness and a can-do spirit that he would like the city to recapture."
— *Asia Times*

"Feng gives a frank and candid recollection of his teenage upbringing in Diamond Hill. The stories he shares with his readers tell all, including sad stories of childhood friends whose futures succumbed to gambling or drug addiction, and the desperate ways in which the poorer townspeople went about making ends meet."
— *Time Out Hong Kong*

"Feng Chi-shun spent his childhood coping with poverty. His memoirs show the value of perseverance, street smarts and good luck."
— *Cairns Media Magazine*

DIAMOND HILL

*Memories of growing up in a
Hong Kong squatter village*

Feng Chi-shun

BLACKSMITH BOOKS

Diamond Hill

ISBN 978-988-17742-4-8

Published by Blacksmith Books
Unit 26, 19/F, Block B, Wah Lok Industrial Centre,
37-41 Shan Mei Street, Fo Tan, Hong Kong
Tel: (+852) 2877 7899
www.blacksmithbooks.com

Typeset in Adobe Garamond by Alan Sargent

First printing November 2009
Second printing February 2011
Third printing September 2013
Fourth printing July 2017

Contents

1950s Kowloon

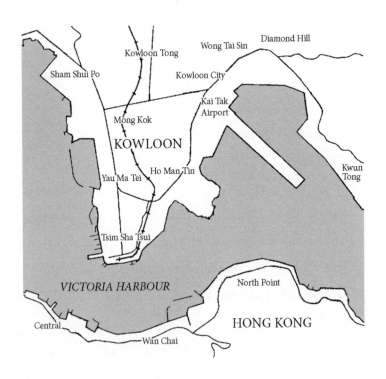

Prologue

M Y FIRST TEN YEARS of life are a bit of a blur. I was born in Hankow (now part of Wuhan in Hubei province), even though my father's ancestors were originally from Zhejiang. The family moved around the country a lot, as did many people during the long years of turmoil and war in China. My mother's family was originally from Chiu Chow in Guangdong, but they too moved about and ended up in Hankow.

The whole family fled communist China when I was a baby. My maternal grandfather was a wealthy man. When we first arrived in Hong Kong, we lived in a two-story house with a big backyard on Humphreys Avenue in Tsim Sha Tsui. My grandfather went back to China after he speculated on gold and lost his fortune overnight. (He lost a million dollars, a humongous amount of money then.) Not long after that, my mother died of meningitis and we moved to

Sham Shui Po, in the same district as Tsung Tsin College secondary school where my father found work as a teacher. My three older sisters and I enrolled in its primary section.

My father remarried, so we needed a bigger home and we moved to Diamond Hill, where the rent was more affordable. Diamond Hill was one of the poorest and most backward of villages in Hong Kong, when Hong Kong was poor and backward. We moved there in 1956 when I was almost ten. I left in 1966 when I was nineteen. During that decade I grew from a boy to a man. Those were the formative years of my life, which made me what I am today. It's a part of my life that I remember well and cherish.

Woody Allen, the American director, worked as a stand-up comedian in his younger days, and one of his routines was to fantasize aloud about living his life backwards. After everyone at his funeral says good things about him, he rises from the dead and goes back to live in the nursing home. He wakes up every morning feeling better than the day before until he becomes so strong he moves out of the home and returns to work. The first day at work, the boss presents him with a gold "retirement" watch. He continues to feel better and stronger every day and when he gets back to his college days, he parties hard and drinks even harder. A pampered childhood is followed by a coddled infancy. Then he turns into a small fetus in a woman's womb, and ends his life with an orgasm.

In spite of that pleasant prospect, I wouldn't want to live my life in reverse order even if I could. I like the idea of feeling younger by the day, but those years in Diamond Hill were harsh and impoverished. Though it was a character-building experience, I am glad it happened in the earlier part of my life and not the later.

This book is mainly drawn from my memory of the time I spent in Diamond Hill. All the places, events and people in the book are real, and I have no reasons to refrain from writing about them. I've had fun writing this memoir, and I'd like to dedicate it to all the inhabitants of Diamond Hill, past and present.

Above: The author and father in Hankow, China, circa 1947

Below: Ah Ho (right) assuming her usual position at the mahjong table

From the smallest
member of the
family in 1953...

...to the tallest ten
years later.

Above: Mabel, anticipating a walk in the countryside

Below: Michael in his favorite chair

Above: In the front yard of the house in Diamond Hill, with stepmother and oldest sister, 1956

Below: Bird's-eye view of the Walled City from Ah Fui's rooftop, 1966

The neighbors and the neighborhood

NOBODY KNEW WHY it was called Diamond Hill. There were certainly no diamond mines, nor diamonds on anyone's fingers. "Diamond" in Chinese can also mean excavation of stones or slate. It felt like a sick joke on the thousands of people there struggling to survive in poverty.

Diamond Hill proper was not that big, but its boundaries were not well-defined, so one could keep walking in any direction for hours and could still find village life. My roaming grounds included Diamond Hill proper and numerous small nearby villages, namely, Sheung Yuen Ling towards the north, Ha Yuen Ling towards the south, Tai Hom Village and Chuk Yuen towards the west, Ngau Chi Wan towards the east, and Tai Koon Yuen towards the northwest. And the surrounding country parks had interesting flora and fauna, hills with narrow trails and streams with water clean enough to drink. The whole area was considered Diamond Hill district by the government.

There was one main road running uphill in the midst of Diamond Hill—a narrow cement thorough-fare which barely allowed one-way traffic for small trucks.

There was a bus stop at the entrance to this main road. On the right side was a bicycle rental shop. I wrecked one of the rental bikes when I first moved there, and hadn't had the guts to face the owner until a couple of years later, when I had a growth spurt and became taller than he was. The first store on the left was a shoe shop. They specialized in hand-made leather dress shoes for men. Not surprisingly, their patrons were mostly from outside the area. Those shoes were not meant for the dusty roads of Diamond Hill.

Not far away on the same side of the shoe store was the famous Wing Lai Yuen Sichuan restaurant with its renowned *dan dan* noodles, the cheapest item on the menu, but still the main draw for people from all over Hong Kong. Legend had it the restaurant didn't cater for take-outs, except for one person alone—Sir Run Run Shaw, who sometimes bestowed the honor of his presence on us in his chauffeured Rolls-Royce on his way to his Clearwater Bay film studio.

The rest of the road was lined with shops of all kinds and packed with hawkers of all trades. There was a Chinese medical practitioner who used to be a barber but hung up his scissors after he claimed to have discovered an ancestral medicine book. He had snakes and baby mice in Chinese wine on exhibit in his shop window. A stationery store was close by. A boy my age looked after the store sometimes. We used to collude on deals in which he sold me stationery with minor defects cheaply so I could pocket the money saved. All the shops were small and single-story. Narrow lanes separating them led to clusters of bungalows and shacks, vegetable fields, and small factories producing handmade goods such as straw hats, cooking utensils, batteries, and Buddhist religious paraphernalia.

Further up was the wet market, occupying the whole road. When a car drove through, all the hawkers would pick up their merchandise and scoot to the side to let the car by. Then all would fall back into their original spots when the car passed. The hawkers guarded their territories with their lives. If a new hawker tried to occupy an earmarked spot, all hell would break loose, and there would be blood.

In the middle of the wet market, the road forked. Bearing left the road led to the Tai Koon Yuen area via a dead-end street called Tai Koon Road with a Baptist church in a wooded area at the very end. Bearing right was a mud road that led to a square. At one corner of the square was a small footpath that turned downhill through vegetable fields and small huts and was an alternative and longer way to the bus stop. Turning further uphill would be the continuation of the Diamond Hill Road.

This road ended when it reached a bridge which led to the Chi Lin nunnery and the Sheung Yuen Ling area where there were rows of upscale apartment blocks, three or four stories high. The one-way road then turned downhill and connected to Hammer Hill Road exiting in the Ngau Chi Wan bus terminal.

Underneath the bridge was a wide stream lined with boulders of various sizes and shapes, but all with smooth surfaces. Households nearby did laundry and washed dishes in the stream, hence the water was not always pristine. But upstream the water was so clear you could count the number of pebbles at the bottom. The shortcut to reach the upstream area was to jump from one boulder to another for half a mile or so uphill, and only the young could manage such a feat. The stream narrowed quite a bit upstream and the boulders were smaller. At one spot, there was a waterfall and the water was deep. That became the swimming pool for boys from all over the area.

We lived in a two-bedroom bungalow half-way up the section of Diamond Hill Road past the square.

It took about twenty minutes to walk home from the bus stop—an inconvenience by today's standards, but we didn't have a choice. There were many who had to walk further and longer. It turned out to be a blessing in disguise. My father lived to be over ninety, even though I had never seen him do any other exercise than this mandatory daily walk.

My father paid for quite a bit of renovations on the house: a Western toilet, a front yard covered by cement, and sides cleared of bushes and dead trees. There was a small back yard which we used as a chicken farm. We reared chickens for their eggs, but they were more trouble than they were worth. Apart from the constant stream of chicken droppings and the smell, the chickens were also susceptible to "chicken plague," which would be today's bird flu. We were soon down to just one chicken, a hardy one which had survived numerous bouts that had killed all her contemporaries. She continued to give us one egg a day for years and years, until she died of old age.

We even had a well in the back, which supplied us with all the water we needed. We fetched the water with a bucket tied to a rope which we tugged while standing astride over the well. After a heavy rainfall, the well would be filled with muddy water almost to the top, and we could scoop water up by bending over and reaching down with an outstretched arm.

The house was small for seven people, the original five plus our new mom and an amah. There was a partition in the kitchen big enough for a small bed for the amah, who stuffed all her earthly possessions under the bed. And I had to make my bed nightly in the living room. There was only one bathroom for all of us to share, and for showers, we used a bucket and a scoop. In winter, we had to wait for boiled water before a shower. All that would seem like unbelievable hardship for people who take modern conveniences for granted, but it was actually an improvement on our accommodation in Sham Shui Po.

There was always some kind of odor. Not far from the house was a wine distillery. The sweet smell of rice wine hung in the air all year round. In the back and to one side was a vegetable field. In late afternoon the farmer irrigated the field with sewage from our septic tank. Luckily, unlike the aroma of wine, the sewage smell didn't linger long enough to ruin our dinner.

The neighbors and the neighborhood

We regularly bought the vegetables harvested by the farmer and sold by his hawker wife in the wet market. Recycling is not a new concept.

On summer nights, it was the scent of anti-mosquito incense burning and the mixture of odors from fauna and flora of the countryside after a hot day.

My family was far from well-to-do, but not in the indigent category. We were "middle class" in a poor neighborhood. There were many wealthier families living in bigger and better flats or village houses, including some British and Portuguese families.

Our next-door neighbor had the biggest and nicest house on the block, with a large landscaped garden and a tall metal front gate. The patriarch of the family was a hoity-toity intellectual. He had two sons, one we nicknamed Chubby because he was slightly over-weight, and the other Skinny because he was not. They were a bit stuck up like the father. Even at that young age, they already had their career paths mapped out, and told us one of them would become a doctor, the other a lawyer.

I was caught gambling in the street by the father, and he told his two sons not to go near me, ever. I didn't blame the father for the ban because I wasn't exactly a model youth. For example, I picked up the smoking habit in my mid-teens. Smoking was widespread and permissible anywhere anytime, including on buses. By then, I was already taller than the average Hong Kong person by a couple of inches, and when I smoked standing up, other people could see what I was doing from the other end of the bus. Who but the father of Skinny and Chubby spotted my transgression and before I reached the stretch of mud path leading back home, my father had already had from him a full account of my misconduct on the bus, plus, I was sure, a recount of all my past conduct unbecoming of a school boy. There was no use lying about it, because as luck would have it, just as I was stepping inside the house, I inadvertently dropped the packet of cigarettes from my coat pocket in front of the whole family. Lucky for me, this happened a few days after the final school examination, in which I performed exceptionally well that year. All was forgiven.

Across the street from us was a row of small two-story shophouses (downstairs a shop, upstairs a residence). At the corner house upstairs lived an older man we nicknamed "the Coughing Man," because he woke up early every morning and spent an hour or so coughing and producing enough phlegm to fill a beer jug. Downstairs was a grocery store owned by a mild-mannered man who never hit me or any other kids when we shoplifted.

Next to the Coughing Man lived a widow and her son, Ah Siu. He pretty much kept to himself. His late father had worked for the Hong Kong Cable & Wireless Company (the predecessor of Hong Kong Telephone Company and PCCW) for years before his death and he might have died while on duty. The company bosses promised the mother that as soon as her son could attain a passing grade in English in the Secondary School Certificate, he would be guaranteed a job. Years later, I went to Cable & Wireless's main office in Tsim Sha Tsui to send a telegraph to the USA, and lo and behold, Ah Siu was behind the counter to attend to my needs.

Another shophouse further down was the home of a drunk, who would send his boy to buy him twenty cents worth of double-distilled rice wine and five cents worth of peanuts just about every evening. When he got drunk, he would prattle on and on until late at night.

Further down the road, there were a few more bungalows. My father's friend Mrs. Chan lived in one of them. Her husband lived in Taiwan and had a prestigious job as a judge. She moved to live in Hong Kong with her two sons and a daughter, so that the two sons could dodge mandatory military service after reaching the age of majority. She brought along a daughter, the least attractive of her three, to serve as a maid to the two boys. We knew all this because she came over to our house often and entertained my father with gossip involving the whole neighborhood and their circle of friends.

Apart from the main road, all access roads in Diamond Hill were narrow lanes or paths crisscrossing all over the place. Houses were built in a random fashion, and were of two types: legal ones built of bricks and mortar, and illegal shanty huts built in whatever space was left.

Because I was forbidden to play with the boys next door, I ventured into the next lane down the road. A boy named Tai Lin was the closest. He had the hardest life of anyone I knew. His father died of tuberculosis when he was eight or nine and his mother, suffering from the disease as well, was unfit to work. They begged from relatives and friends to survive. His mother would bring him along for the begging expeditions. He had occasional meals at a relative's home, where he would be hit on the knuckles with chopsticks by the older sons of the family for going after food without prior permission. He was made to go through numerous humiliations at a young age, such as kneeling in front of people, often to no avail. He ended up being a nervous wreck of a young man with little self-esteem. But I admire him for his fortitude; he was never broken. He survived, with a vengeance, in spite of being everyone's punching bag.

He was devoted to his two younger brothers, and had often made sacrifices for them. For example, even though he could have strived for better for himself after secondary school, given that he was college material, he took up a training post at one of the education colleges because they paid a better salary than most other jobs. He needed the extra money to support the two brothers. He sent them to the US for higher education, and subsequently, one became a doctor, the other a successful businessman.

But life wasn't so rosy for him. His home was a tin shack shared with an old couple. The front door was so flimsy it could be kicked open by a child. There was no privacy to speak of; people walked in and out while they were changing clothes.

His mother was a loud-mouthed ill-tempered bitter woman whose idea of motherhood was to constantly criticize her children. Tai Lin put up with all that without a fight, and his escape was to grab one of his favorite books and read it aloud, especially during his mother's long-winded tirades about his inadequacies.

I went to his house often just to hang out. But if I heard Tai Lin reading aloud inside when I approached the hut, I would avoid the place like the plague.

In the nearby brick house, there was another father-less boy named Ah Bok. He spoke Cantonese with a Fujian accent, and that immediately got him branded as retarded. I liked him because he was a friendly and kind boy who had a perpetual smile, and he laughed loudly at my lame jokes. He was so even-tempered no one could get a rise out of him, except a boy called Umbrella, so named because his real name was similar to an umbrella company. For a while, Umbrella made Ah Bok's life miserable by constant bullying and harassing. Instead of fighting back, which would have been futile because Ah Bok was half his tormentor's size, he asked his mother to befriend Umbrella's mother, and the two families had meals together a few times. The rule was that if the parents were friends, the children were as well. Umbrella had no choice but to stop bothering Ah Bok.

Umbrella was one of the few boys around with both parents, but that did not render him well adjusted. He was restless and reckless, making him both excit-ing and dangerous to be with. He led me astray many times, by committing the usual teenage pranks and petty crimes.

He went to school at La Salle College, and attained his biggest claim to fame during that water rationing period in 1963. It was serious rationing, something like four hours of water supply every fourth day, and it was so tight housewives stopped buying food items that required water to prepare and cook, such as vegetables. People would book trips to Macau to have showers there.

Umbrella had the balls to sneak into the formidable headmaster's private quarters in La Salle to take a bath, using the headmaster's clean towels to dry off afterwards. He was caught, but became a legend.

Further down the lane was a boy named Ah Noun, which means "girly" in the Chiu Chow dialect. A lot of Chiu Chow families named their sons Ah Noun because they believed girls were hardier, and would have a better chance of surviving childhood diseases. Ah Noun was no girly; he was the village bully. Although fatherless, Ah Noun had numerous Chiu Chow "uncles" visiting him regularly. We could always tell there had been such a visit because Ah Noun would don a slick haircut, have some money in his pocket, and walk around with an attitude and a swagger. Years later, Tai Lin told me that he had had to pay Ah Noun fifty cents a week for protection while living in Diamond Hill. Ah Noun became a policeman later in life.

There was a small movie studio at the end of the lane. The owner's son was quite a bit older than we were and we thought he was the coolest dude on the planet. He never said much but always had a cigarette dangling from the side of his mouth. He was always unshaven, disheveled and his eyes were always half-closed. Rumor had it he never slept because of numerous work orders for film editing which frequently required him to pull an all-nighter. Once in a while, he would dump some discarded films at our feet, and told us how difficult his job was. We used the films to make wallets and other useless artifacts. Or we set them on fire for fun because they were highly inflammable.

The cool movie guy had a thing going with that woman who occupied a room next to Ah Bok's. He was her frequent visitor when her "husband" wasn't around. She had her window curtain drawn all year round, and Ah Bok claimed to hear moans coming from her room lasting for hours whenever she was visited by Mr. Cool.

Ah Bok's building was full of such "single" women. They didn't work. A few times a year, each woman would get all dolled up for a male visitor, who would stay for the night and had his own slippers and pajamas ready for him. All the men seemed to have the same occupation—working on a ship, and that conveniently explained their long spells of absence.

That was just the first lane down the road, and there were scores of other lanes down the stretch, and I had been to most of them. Those lanes branched out into other lanes, but you could count on one or two of them leading to the next village and beyond. There were countless boys there that I got to know and play with occasionally, but Tai Lin, Ah Bok, Umbrella, and Ah Noun were the boys I ran into all the time, because they were close neighbors.

Even though I was not aware of it then, there was little community spirit in Diamond Hill. It was partly Chinese pathos, and partly refugee mentality. Diamond Hill to most was a temporary home, a stepping stone until something better came along. One of our neighbors went into the garment business and as soon as he had it made, he and his family moved to Hong Kong Island, without even saying goodbye. Ah Bok's mother inherited some money from a relative, and they moved to North Point. Even Tai Lin moved away after working as a teacher for a few years and having saved enough money for the down payment for a small flat in one of the MTR developments. Umbrella and his family migrated to the United Kingdom to start up a restaurant business, as soon as their papers were ready. Ah Noun moved away too; well, he went to jail. My family moved to Ho Man Tin when my father got a higher-paying job with the American Consulate, without compunction. I moved away even earlier, to a hostel of Hong Kong University in my freshman year, and never looked back.

I was the only boy and the lowest in the totem pole in our household. Naturally, I was the designated errand boy. I did not like the chores and the best way to avoid them was not to be around. I was seldom home. If I thought I had worn out my welcome in the company of Tai Lin or Ah Bok or Umbrella or anyone else, I would go up the hills to find a trail for a walk and a daydreaming session. In the hot summer days there were the streams along the trails, where we boys could frolic and do what boys do when there is plenty of water around.

There was always some kind of action in the square down the road, and the Chi Lin Nunnery in Sheung Yuen Ling, the Catholic church around the corner, and the Baptist church up in Tai Koon Road, were all open to the public for free. There were even movie studios in Diamond Hill. Then there were games to play; and the gambling. So much to do, so little time.

Bus stops

I USED THAT SAME BUS ROUTE thousands of times. The buses were numbers 7 and 9, double-deckers with the Kowloon Motor Bus logo, yellow and red paint outside, and green metallic benches inside. I think they are running more or less the same routes today, but in those days there was no such thing as air-conditioning, and each bus was manned by four people: In addition to the driver, there were the conductor and two fare collectors. The driver didn't have to deal with commuters and he was paid a little more than the others. The fare collectors, one on each deck, walked up and down the aisle carrying a canvas bag to collect ten cents from children and twenty cents from adults in exchange for a ticket. The canvas bag got to be quite heavy by the end of the trip, and God forbid if you happened to have no small change and only a ten-dollar bill—he would unload ninety-nine ten-cent coins on you with a smirk.

The conductor was always the burliest of the four. His job was to guard the exit gate at the back, and he signaled to the driver by pulling a thin rope connected to a bell in the front near the driver's seat. One ring meant someone needed to get off at the next stop; two rings meant it would be safe to drive off again. He had to determine how many commuters were to be allowed in at each bus stop. Not an easy job during rush hours when, with bus already full, ten to twenty commuters would push and shove, and literally gate-crash into the bus. He had to deal with a lot of arguments and fights. I had seen rogue characters pull him off the bus and challenge him to a fistfight, and later summon a few tough guys to ambush him at the bus terminal.

Umbrella had an argument with a conductor, and he made threats to ambush the conductor at the Ngau Chi Wan bus depot. He didn't have tough guys at his beck and call, so he tricked some of his friends, me included, into gathering around the depot at a certain hour with the promise of free beer and food. While the five of us were standing there, waiting to go for beer, Umbrella made a spectacle of himself going around the bus depot demanding to see that conductor, and acted real disappointed when the station master told him that it was his day off. Later, Umbrella confessed that he had known that beforehand.

Umbrella was able to save face, the conductor was sort of taught a lesson, and we had our free beer and food without lifting a finger.

The Kowloon Motor Bus workers were no angels either, all rough and wily. They were also my first tutors of the colorful Cantonese dialect. When the bus was not busy, they would gather around the driver, and the conversation, littered with foul words, would usually be about their craftiness in committing and getting away with scams and petty crimes. For instance, the driver would boast that he had ways to jam the engine of the bus, and he would do it whenever he felt like having a break. The fare collector would egg him on, claiming to have won at mahjong the night before, and had enough money to treat them all to some beer if the driver could give them all the rest of the day off. The conductor liked to brag about the finer points of committing frotteurism on female commuters while making it look accidental. He also claimed the cute young thing he molested the previous morning had seemed to enjoy it, and on their next encounter, he might even consider asking her out.

That was how I got to learn all the Cantonese swear words at a young age. Sex education was unknown, but I was at least schooled in the necessary basic vocabulary.

Getting an education in swearing aside, the bus ride was an important part of my young life because it connected my life in school and the one at home. The bus stops compartmentalized my life into different facets.

Buses 7 and 9 both ran along Waterloo Road before turning into Prince Edward Road and stopped close to La Salle College where I went to school. The La Salle stop was the unofficial gathering place for an arranged fight between two La Salle students. La Salle boys were infamous for being thuggish. "I'll wait for you at the bus stop" was the usual threat of a bully. When it was time, a "student leader" would show up to conduct the duel. The leader was usually someone older, and had repeated a few grades so that he had classmates, new and old, spanning several years. He would lead the procession consisting of the two fighters and a group of spectators to a park or playground nearby. He also laid down the ground rules, such as: three rounds, three minutes each, and no kicking once the opponent was down. But these were not real fights. We knew no one would get seriously hurt.

Real fights were spontaneous, and usually involved weapons. They were scary, because, fueled by testosterone and the "face" thing, no one ever backed down. There would be blood. I've lost count of the number of fights I witnessed there, but I remember a particularly vicious one involving someone I was friendly with. He was on the short side but stocky. His opponent was tall and lanky. They were whispering to each other and all of a sudden, their faces turned pale. Someone let out a loud scream followed by profanity and fists started to fly. The tall guy came prepared, and he was able to quickly pull off his belt with a big steel buckle, which he started to rain on the short guy. Soon blood was dripping down the short guy's face, but the tall one still wouldn't let up. The short guy then reached into the pocket of his trousers, and someone yelled: "He has a knife." And the tall guy ran like hell in the direction of Waterloo Road. When color returned to his face, the short guy came over to me and told me that would be the last time he left home without a knife. This guy is now working for the FBI in the US.

Sometimes, the students involved in the fights were never seen again, because the penalty for fighting, especially for repeat offenders, was expulsion from school.

Waterloo Road in those days had a wide and deep ditch acting as the dividing median for the wide road. The ditch had lots of water in it, and all sorts of debris including an occasional automobile, especially after heavy rainfall or a typhoon. It ran through the heart of Kowloon Tong, a wealthy area where there were detached houses with landscaped gardens, private car parks, and a side entrance for uniformed servants to use. Female servants, called amahs, working in those households wore black baggy pants and white *cheong-sam* tops. There were also uniformed male servants working as gardeners and chauffeurs.

Waterloo Road intersected with Boundary Street, Prince Edward Road and Argyle Street, all lined with trees and buildings known as *yeung lau* which meant "Western buildings." These were high rises, ten to twenty stories high, stylish and with elevators, gardens, and car parks. In general, people who lived in *yeung lau* were quite well-off.

When I was in La Salle College, I used to hang out at the bus stop on Waterloo Road, even though it was in the opposite direction from home. Near the stop was a confectionery store where girls from the Maryknoll Convent School—an all-girl Catholic school—also hung out. While waiting for buses, they were also waiting for La Salle boys to gawk at them or maybe to chat them up.

Not that it ever did me any good. The boys going home in that direction lived in the wealthier parts of town. All of them seemed to have clear skin, silky hair, money in their pockets, and a La Salle school tie to show off. As for me, I had only the tie. It was a "cool" thing to do all the same, pretending to belong to the "in" crowd. It would also lend more credence to my lies when I boasted to other hapless classmates about a certain Maryknoll girl eyeing me.

Another La Salle boy in my class, who lived in the Tai Koon Yuen area in Diamond Hill, fell in love with a pretty and bashful Maryknoll girl, but she wasn't particularly interested in him. That didn't stop him from trying. He woke up early every morning and traveled by bus to her home in Tsim Sha Tsui and waited at her bus stop, took the bus with her to her school before continuing on to La Salle. And he repeated the routine on her way home. He "took" her to school and back home every school day and talked to her continuously, but she only bowed her head all the way, and never seemed to respond. He kept that up for years. He should probably have got a medal for perseverance, for he sure didn't get the girl. My sister knew her. After high school, she found a job as a flight attendant. She was not shy any more, became a party girl, and preferred dating older Western men. The La Salle boy was heartbroken, and I don't know what happened to him next. He didn't do well in school, understandably, considering the amount of time wasted on bus rides all those years.

Traveling eastbound after La Salle College, the next stop was Kowloon City. My friend Ah Fui lived in that area. Some days, I would stop by there on my way home. We played stupid games on his rooftop, such as kicking and chasing after a plastic toy, or if we had two coins to rub against each other, we played a gambling game—the poor trying to rob the poor. But that was nothing to write home about. What was most memorable were our ventures into the Walled City, despite stern warnings not to do so from all grown-ups around us. That's what teenage hormones could do to teenage brains. There is a separate chapter on my adventures there.

Kowloon City was so-called because it was where the Walled City was situated. Outside the Walled City, there were mostly low-rise apartment blocks and shops instead of the village houses and tin shacks in villages close by. It was basically like a big wet market and today's Ladies' Street combined. Things one could not find in other parts of Kowloon would be sold in Kowloon City. It was a place to go for bargain hunting. We even saw the occasional Caucasian women picking up stuff from the roadside hawkers. Ah Fui told me they were White Russians living in the area.

The low-rise buildings in Kowloon City were the typical *tong lau,* or "Chinese buildings." They were basic low-rise match-box shaped utilitarian buildings with a wide stairwell and no elevator. Architects then had not found a way to design a building along a road without wide pillars in all corners. So every shop had two large square columns in front where the name of the shop would be painted. It was possible because Chinese characters can run vertically as well as horizontally. Unlike Kowloon Tong and areas around Waterloo Road, Kowloon City was a poor neighborhood. For instance, Ah Fui's family of three lived in a small room on the fifth floor of a *tong lau,* sharing the flat with four other families.

Continuing eastbound, there was a long stretch between Kowloon City and the next stop: Wong Tai Sin. Kowloon City and the areas before it, such as Kowloon Tong, Ho Man Tin, Mong Kok, Jordan, Tsim Sha Tsui and Sham Shui Po, were considered the older and urban part of Kowloon. Wong Tai Sin and beyond were considered rural and undeveloped. The bus route from Kowloon City to the bus terminal at Ngau Chi Wan was monotonous, as for the whole length there was on one side the fence bordering the Kai Tak Airport compound, and on the other a wide drainage ditch with a stone embankment several feet tall.

Wong Tai Sin is famous for being the home of the temple bearing the same name. It was the biggest and most frequented temple in Kowloon. On Buddhist holy days, thousands of devotees would go there, armed with incense sticks, paper offerings and food, to worship their favorite gods, and more importantly, to pray so that wishes were granted and dreams realized.

Following Wong Tai Sin and continuing towards east was Chuk Yuen, a nondescript and sparsely populated village. Then another small village called Tai Hom.

In the earlier years, right before Tai Hom Village, there was a barricade across the road similar to a train level crossing. Except this one was for planes to use an intersecting runway. The planes were small and carried one or two people. By the time our bus stopped, the plane would already be out of its hangar and turned around facing the open space towards the sea, the wings seeming to flutter in the wind. As the plane accelerated along the runway, it rocked until it lifted into the sky. My father told me those were military planes. Watching them take off provided some form of entertainment for commuters, until after umpteen times, it became a nuisance.

That runway was abandoned with the expansion of Kai Tak Airport. The hangar was left locked and deserted, and the vacant space in front of it was turned into a makeshift football pitch for some years.

The next stop was Diamond Hill, where I got off.

The bus ride took half an hour but seemed like an eternity to me. Only when I had to walk home because I had either lost the bus fare or spent it on snacks did I appreciate its convenience. When I became older and bolder, I learned from a friend that if you invoked a name, the fare collector would let you ride for free. It cost me fifty cents to pry the name out of him but it was money well spent.

The magic words were "I am Lui Wah-ying's people." Lui Wah-ying was one of the founders of Kowloon Motor Bus. The fact that I got off at Diamond Hill, a squatter area for refugees, making no sense for Mr. Lui's relatives, did not deter me from carrying out the ploy. The trick was to look and speak confidently.

The first time I cashed in on my investment I actually had money in my pocket. I figured the worst that could happen was for me to cough up the fare and be embarrassed for the duration of the bus ride. The bus was not full. I positioned myself in a corner so that the chances of other commuters overhearing me were slim. When the collector came, I cocked my head, looked him in the eyes, and said the magic words in a calm and firm voice. He hesitated for a second or two, nodded, and walked away. I said hallelujah.

Hong Kong in the 50s and 60s was a city of dirt-poor refugees, who had fled post-war hardship or communist rule in Mainland China. A minority were luckier and brought with them wealth and business know-how. And in the case of the garment industry owners, expensive machinery was transferred from big cities in China such as Shanghai to restart the business in Hong Kong.

There was a constant stream of refugees sneaking across the border illegally, causing an acute shortage of homes. Villages along this bus route provided refuge for the poorest of the poor. Then friends and relatives came to join them, causing the population to grow like wildfire. Unlike today, when being a new immigrant from Mainland China is looked down upon, everyone then was assumed to be an immigrant, and no questions would be asked about how one arrived.

Paying jobs were hard to come by, but willingness to work was never a problem. The big Chiu Chow boy who lived across from us cleared the shrubs and weeds from the sides of our house for us, and my stepmother was able to bargain his pay down to fifty cents for three to four hours of hard work.

In the 50s and 60s, Hong Kong became the world capital for plastic flowers and garments. Someone told my sisters and me that we could make some money doing a summer job at home working with plastic flowers and the pay would be two dollars per bushel. We jumped at the opportunity to make the extra cash, even though we were not exactly starving. That was the mindset of the whole community at that time.

I was twelve or thirteen then and I worked non-stop for weeks to attach plastic green leaves and red flowers onto plastic stems with metal wires inside. The joy came at the end of each day when we counted the number of bushels ready to go.

When I was older, I worked summer months as a packer at a family friend's garment factory in Lai Chi Kok. My job was to sort out dress shirts of the same color and fabric, and pack them into cardboard boxes before sealing them with adhesive tape and labeling them. Shirts with buttoned-down collars were the big thing then, and I had to make sure the regular-collar ones were separated from the buttoned ones. I was fifteen or sixteen, but not by far the youngest person working there. There were hordes of younger girls who worked as seamstresses. And even though their work required more skill, I was told they were paid less than me, because they were girls.

My job was not exactly tough, but the foreman kept messing with my head by giving us deadlines. He would announce a date for a particularly large shipment order, only to push it back a week, over and over again, until he lost all credibility and we would just do things at our own pace, no matter what he had said. And then the big boss came out and told us the real deadline, and we busted our butts and did overtime, only to find out the "real" deadline was another week later.

We knew for sure it was the real thing when the foreman was being hands-on, and was filling up boxes with waste paper and sealing them. He told us we were allowed a ten percent margin of error.

We made the deadline, and celebrated the occasion with a meal followed by a poker game. I held on to my money for dear life. No way was I going to blow it after toiling for it for two long months.

After I was finished with the Secondary School Certificate Examination, I started to work as a private tutor to younger kids. My customers were usually well-off families living close to La Salle. It was a better way to make money than handling plastic flowers and garments. I was respected and even admired because I was a La Salle boy and I had been moderately successful in the Secondary School Certificate Examination. I needed the money because I was starting to go out with girls, not to mention gambling and drinking, and the income I made from tutoring was timely because by then my spending habits outstripped many times over the pocket money from my father. I had my first taste of having a white-collar job.

The local saying: "we all grew up under Lion Rock," which describes grassroots people of Hong Kong, was especially apt for people who lived along that bus route. From Waterloo Road to Diamond Hill and all the bus stops in between, Lion Rock loomed in the background tall and mighty. The summit looked more like a lion then than today. Fifty years of wind and rain must have caused a lot of attrition to its facial features.

I was fortunate and proud to be someone who grew up under Lion Rock.

Schools

WHEN MY FATHER FOUND WORK as a teacher in Tsung Tsin College in Sham Shui Po, he put me in the primary section of the same school out of convenience. He didn't expect me to become a source of embarrassment for him.

I was a daydreamer and never paid attention in class. I was also too lazy to do any homework. At the end of the school year, there would be a final examination, and all students were ranked according to the total of their scores in different subjects. They handed out the report cards in a descending order of merit. The top students were given their report cards first and they received applause. It would take a long time for my turn. I was grateful there was always one student even worse off than me, though being second last still meant failure and having to repeat the grade.

Being promoted to the next grade was by the effort of my father, who used his influence as a teacher to beg the principal to give me another chance to straighten myself out. The begging at the end of each year became a ritual. He had to do it four years in a row.

I was "promoted" to grade five the year we moved to Diamond Hill, and was transferred to Tsung Tsin College, the English medium and secondary section of the school system run by the same church. The school campus was located on Tai Po Road close to the junction of Nathan Road and Boundary Street. As a teacher there, my father figured he could provide me with more supervision, since all my teachers were his colleagues and friends. It was an awkward situation for me because no matter what I did, I would get a double dose of attention.

The school's surroundings were more sunny and bright than the old school. The campus was not the only thing bright and sunny. The form teacher was a cute young lady called Miss Yau. She was petite and curvaceous, especially in her colorful *cheongsam* and heels which she wore most days. She always had make-up on and a splash of perfume. When she talked, I was mesmerized by the way her red lips moved and the dimples on her cheeks appeared and disappeared. I started to pay attention in class and do my homework to please her. For her to look in my direction, call out my name, or pat my head would make my head spin for days on end.

What a difference a pretty teacher made! When they handed out report cards in mid-term that year, I was one of the first. When I showed my report card to my father, he didn't believe it and wondered aloud if I had cheated in the exam. But he soon found out it was for real because he didn't have to beg anyone anymore to promote me at the end of the year.

Part of the reason why I could rebound so quickly from the bottom to the top of the class was that the school was not full of high achievers. Many students were a few years older than I was, a situation tolerated in the school system in that era. I was prepubescent and it was weird to have classmates who grew beards and were rumored to have children of their own. Many of them were recent immigrants who had never had much schooling prior to enrolling in the school. They might also have been afflicted with all kinds of learning disorders. It was like—in the kingdom of the blind, the one-eyed man is king. Anyone semi-intelligent could be a top scorer in that rinky-dink school.

Our neighbor Mrs. Chan, the gossip monger, asked my father what he had done to turn me into a good student and what he could do to make her younger son do well in school. They tossed around all kinds of theories for why I had suddenly become such a good student. They never guessed it was the crush on a young woman which did the trick.

The obsession of parents for their children to do well in school was palpable. Mrs. Chan came over and talked about her son's poor school performance for hours on end, boring my father to tears. A classmate, also the son of a teacher, had been top of the class since kindergarten, but when he was in my class that year, he faltered and did not make the top ten in the final examination. There was such a fuss over the matter his father requested a review of the marking procedures of all his papers.

While I was starting to get a little respect at home, my social life had also improved dramatically. I hadn't had any friends in the old school, and then suddenly I started to have lots of friends whom I met in Miss Yau's class. We had at least one thing in common: we were all in love with our teacher.

Miss Yau organized activities after school for us but attendance was not mandatory. They were usually social gatherings for boys and girls such as group singing, and games like musical chairs and Simon Says. There were the same diehards attending, seven or eight of us boys and a few girls. The boys were interested only in Miss Yau and not those girls.

One of the boys was Ah Fui from Kowloon City, who was a slight boy with thick glasses. Ah Fui's way of getting attention from Miss Yau was to smile at her non-stop like a moron. He was polite and mild-mannered and you would never have guessed the voracious appetite and capacity for food of that pint-sized body. While we played mahjong when older, he would devour half a loaf of bread washed down with coffee made with sweetened condensed milk. A couple of hours later, it would be dinner time, and he would shovel three big bowls of rice down his throat. Then a few hours later, he would be asking for late-night snacks. He lived with his mother and a baby brother. He actually had a father, but saw him only once every few years because the father and some older children were busy eking out a living in a faraway and backward town in Panama, and returning home to visit any more often (by ship) would be too wasteful of money and time. Ah Fui's appetite was not confined to food. He and I were partners-in-crime when we went over to the Walled City in our early teens to have a taste of pornography.

Another boy, Ah Lai, had two giant moles on his face, one on the forehead and the other on the nose. His way of attracting Miss Yau's attention was to do cartwheels and jump around like a monkey in front of her. The moles dominated his facial features so much that people often didn't bother with his real name and simply addressed him as Dai Mak ("Big Mole"). He was voted among us the least likely to commit a crime, for good reason (imagine him in a police line-up). We found camaraderie during recess when together we visited the fish-ball stand in the school cafeteria. That place was always jam-packed with kids waving their coins in the air and shouting to place an order. Ah Lai would stand close to the stand and do his bidding while I hid behind him and reached out with a toothpick to help myself to the fish balls for free. When I was done feeding my face, we would trade places. I forget who came up with the idea, but the first time we did it, we left that place rolling on the ground with laughter, stuffed with fish balls up to our eyeballs and yet still holding on to our only ten-cent coins.

There was Ah Yuk, nicknamed "Grammar King" for his English proficiency. Ah Yuk often asked Miss Yau questions about English grammar that were way over our head, and we hated him for all the attention he was getting. He loved Western music, table tennis, and girls, in that order. Ah Yuk's mother was a concubine and a widow. But her late husband had made sure she would be taken care of. She owned the flat she lived in, and she rented out two rooms and lived off the rent and her savings. She had never worked in her whole life and had a *mui tsai*—a "lady-in-waiting" following her around and doing all the housework. She didn't allow Ah Yuk or his younger sister Anita to do any housework either. Years later, I found out Ah Yuk had never used a hammer or a screwdriver his whole life. Ah Yuk's mother was the most hospitable person in the world. We had many meals in her house over the years. Every Christmas, we had dance parties in their living room, with Ah Yuk supplying the music and Anita supplying the girls.

Lau Lee-hok came from a wealthy family, even though there was no way we could tell then. He was chauffeured to school daily but asked the driver to drop him off one block away so that he could "walk" to school like the rest of the students. His family, we found out in later years, was the biggest maker of jeans in the world, and owned blocks of properties near Yau Yat Chuen. Lau Lee-hok was polite, well-behaved and modest—a perfect boy. He was Miss Yau's favorite and we were all envious of him.

Ng Hon-ming, whose father was a taxi driver, tried to draw Miss Yau's attention by being naughty. He often used chalk to coat the side of his desk, knowing Miss Yau liked to lean on it while reading out loud to us. He then drew our attention to the chalk marks on Miss Yau's *cheongsam* around her hips and sniggered. Miss Yau would frown at him for being bad and that was good enough for him. He was not very smart with the books but was street-smart. One day, he offered to make me a special friend. He took me to a secret site on the hillside next to the school campus, which he said he had done research on for days and had determined to be the best spot for the ceremony. I was almost moved to tears by his efforts and sincerity. We knelt together facing each other. Then he made me raise my right hand while he did the same, and both of us were sworn to brotherhood in eternity. That was fine. But I found out later that the scoundrel had done the same thing to all his classmates.

Lee Yat-wah was one or two years older and was bigger than we were for the first couple of years, and he bullied us. The most victimized person was Ah Yuk, who was as meek and timid as a lamb. Whenever Lee Yat-wah had lost money gambling with us, he would take it out on Ah Yuk by punching his stomach, once for every ten cents lost. Then we outgrew him and he immediately changed tack and started to fawn over us. He was one shrewd operator, and the most parsimonious person I had ever known. Whenever we went to restaurants, we would ask him to be in charge of ordering food, because he could strike the best deal for us. He tried to act real innocent in the presence of Miss Yau, but we didn't think she was fooled.

One other boy, Cheung Ka-leung, was a funny guy; he made Miss Yau laugh by being goofy. His biggest problem was that he had always performed poorly in school examinations. It baffled me because he appeared as intelligent as any of us, but when it was time for the school to hand out report cards, he would be absent for fear of embarrassment. His parents would have already gotten his report card for him privately. In retrospect, he probably suffered from dyslexia, which might have explained his clownish behavior as a front.

After Miss Yau's class, we became life-long friends. In later years, Ah Yuk and I transferred to La Salle College; Ah Fui and Lau Lee-hok transferred to Wah Yan College; and Ah Lai went to Maryknoll Fathers' School. The others were not as good academically and continued on in Tsung Tsin or some similarly low-caliber schools. We went our separate ways, but we have kept in touch over the years. We still meet once in a while to have a meal or to play mahjong, more than fifty years after we first met. We still talk about Miss Yau.

Tsung Tsin was a Christian school and discipline was the order of the day. There was Ms. Shum, an old spinster who insisted on being called Madam Shum. She dressed herself the same way every day of the year, in a long sky-blue cotton *cheongsam,* which didn't hug the body like Miss Yau's. She also wore white stockings and black shoes all year round. She was fanatically religious, and her mission in life was to punish naughty boys. She would dish out punishments to boys at the drop of a hat, including corporal ones such as hitting the palm with a ruler, her favorite. When she was dishing this out, she would become real emotional and her face would turn beefy red. The older boys called her "Old Abalone" and I had never understood why until I was older and had a chance to have a good look at one.

I got into trouble with her once for throwing wet toilet paper up at the ceiling, and not only did I get my hands whipped, I also got an earful from my father because he too got a lecture from Madam Shum.

After Miss Yau, we had a Mrs. Wong as our form teacher, a kind, matronly woman who sacrificed her private hours to give us after-class extra-curricular activities such as singing contests and social outings. The next year, our form teacher was a pretentious man who had greasy hair and wore a bow-tie all year round.

He tried to show off his wealth by awarding money to the best scorers of his weekly tests. We all knew he was just trying to impress Miss Yau. Then the following year we had an older form teacher whose nickname was the "Praying Man," so called because of his monotonous mumblings in the classroom. Staying awake was our biggest challenge.

I continued to do well in school even though I wasn't in Miss Yau's class any more, because by then I was addicted to academic success and the prestige that came with it.

During the four years in Tsung Tsin College I had to commute back and forth between Sham Shui Po and Diamond Hill. I dreaded it, especially since most of my friends lived close by the school. But all I had was energy. I would stay behind after school to run around before I went back home to Diamond Hill to run around some more.

The La Salle College bus stop was on the way home. And those La Salle boys sure looked smart in the school uniform and tie. Quite a few of them used the same bus as I did, and when they got off at Diamond Hill, they walked uphill along that one-way cement road, proud as peacocks.

In the summer of 1960, a friend told me about La Salle College recruiting new Form Two students. I rushed over to fill in an application form. An examination was scheduled for us. Two weeks later, we went back to see if our names were on the list. I had tears of joy on that day.

It was a fateful day for me because La Salle was a top Catholic secondary school on Kowloon side. The school campus was magnificent. It was huge compared to what I was used to. It had a cathedral with a dome next to the main building where all the classrooms were, a large soccer field surrounded by running tracks, two basketball and two tennis courts. There were steps and a driveway in a wooded area leading to Boundary Street.

Even though I did not have those things in mind then, transferring to La Salle was a stepping stone to Hong Kong University and a comfortable future. I morphed from a bottom-of-the-barrel schoolboy in Sham Shui Po to a star student in Diamond Hill.

There were few students going to Tsung Tsin who lived in Diamond Hill. Tsung Tsin was nothing to brag about, and that school's requirement of wearing a school badge or tie was not strictly enforced. Nobody took notice of me until I started wearing the La Salle school tie.

All elite schools in those days were run by Christian organizations and Western educators. Westerners in the teaching staff of a school automatically made it elite. These schools were better funded and better equipped, and had more posh school campuses. They attracted the *crème de la crème* of students; hence their results in the School Certificate Examination were better. Success breeds success.

There were only three elite boys' schools on Kowloon side: La Salle, Wah Yan, and Diocesan. There were quite a number of La Salle boys in Diamond Hill, but few from Wah Yan and Diocesan.

The general opinion was that La Salle boys were thuggish, Wah Yan boys gentlemanly, and Diocesan boys debonair. That sort of explained why so many La Salle boys came from Diamond Hill.

I knew of only one family with Wah Yan boys, the Fung brothers, John, Robert and George. They, like their father, were sharp dressers and used lots of grease in their hair. The father was distinguished looking with a mustache. The winter uniform for Wah Yan boys was a green blazer. Those brothers had, instead of just one school blazer like the rest of us, numerous ones in different shades of green. The father and the three sons were all the same size and I knew for a fact they shared their wardrobes, so they had four times the number of clothes to show off.

The only Diocesan boys I knew were Chubby and Skinny, our next-door neighbors. By the way, that debonair thing I just talked about, there were exceptions.

All school kids from the Diamond Hill area gathered at the same bus stop every morning on the way to school. From the uniforms and ties, we knew who went to which school. Boys who went to schools other than the famous three looked up to us. We were perceived to be elite students, and would have a bright future.

The significance of having enrolled in an elite school was not lost on my parents' friends, who would encourage their own children to become my friends, quite a turnaround for a lowly Tsung Tsin boy who had been forbidden to play with Chubby and Skinny in case their chances of becoming a doctor or a lawyer would be ruined.

The caliber of the students at La Salle was more than a cut above Tsung Tsin. I had to study a lot harder just to be above average. My first year there, I had a classmate named Leung Pang-wai whose Chinese essays were frequently read out loud by the teacher in class. His writings were more like those from adult literati than a thirteen-year-old boy. Another boy named Chan Kam-shing was good in every subject, and was the top boy hands down. These boys did nothing but bury themselves in homework and text-books, unheard of in Tsung Tsin. There were foreign nationals in the school, including Portuguese, Indian, American Chinese, Vietnamese, and the occasional British. They were native English speakers, as were many of the teachers who were La Salle Christian Brothers who had vowed poverty, chastity and obed-ience to the order, and devotion to educational work for poor and needy boys. It was quite intimidating to be among people who spoke only English and no Chinese. The standard of English was much higher than what I was used to.

Science and mathematics were my favorite subjects in Tsung Tsin, but I found out soon enough I was no genius after I had seen what some of my classmates could do. It became even harder in the higher grades when students of comparable abilities were put together in the same class.

There were cliques. The top boys hung together, and so did the top jocks. There were also the few goody-two-shoe boys who were ideal young men in the eyes of teachers, and they became prefects. And naturally, they were unpopular among the rest of the students.

The most popular students were those with girl-friends, because there would always be the prospect of a double date coming someone's way. If that happened, you would hear them talk about it in detail for weeks. But most of us had no such luck. Among other things, very few of us had the money to take a girl out for a date. We heard horror stories about boys being dumped because all they could afford was taking walks along the seafront. On the other hand, we heard that one classmate, a Eurasian boy with an Elvis Presley hairdo, took a girl out to the Hilton Hotel's Eagle's Nest for dinner and spent more than a hundred dollars there in one night. That kind of story was enough to make us think twice before even trying to ask anyone to arrange a blind date.

There was bullying, but nothing treacherous or sadistic. Every student, including the bullies, valued being a La Salle boy, and didn't want to be expelled. There were petty crimes, usually involving vandalism and theft. A classmate of mine lost his school bag after school while playing football. He got a severe scolding from his parents but was given some money to buy used books to replace the ones stolen. He went down to Mong Kok to a store specializing in used books, and lo and behold, he found his own books on the shelf for sale.

I had made friends while studying in La Salle, but they were never as close as those from Tsung Tsin and Diamond Hill. Partly it was because they were not childhood friends, but mostly it was because of the competitive nature of those school years, be it in sports, examination results, girls, and every other aspect of a young man's formative years.

The teachers at La Salle were more colorful than those in Tsung Tsin. It was an all-boys school and there were no female teachers to give a soft touch to the teaching process. The atmosphere was harsh and disciplinarian, full of machismo and one-upmanship. The headmaster was Brother Felix and his title was Director. He was formidable because he held the power to expel us, and allegedly was the only one in the school authorized to dish out corporal punishment. But during my years there, I had never seen or heard of him giving any student corporal punishment, he simply kicked them out of the school. On the other hand, our physical education tutor, nicknamed "Coolie" because of his build and demeanor, chased after us and gave us karate chops to the neck whenever we pissed him off.

Many of our teachers were De La Salle brothers from the United Kingdom, and that automatically inspired awe. They were dedicated, hardworking and were generally well-liked. Most of the Chinese teachers had an attitude, perhaps for survival, since they had to deal with many unruly students.

In my first year there, the form teacher was Mr. Cheung, who was always grumpy and cynical. In retrospect, I suspect he was a tippler, because at regular intervals, he would complain of headaches and would tell us to read on our own so that he could rest. The next year, we had the meek and handsome Mr. Chan with long wavy hair. He was somewhat deaf and constantly played with his hearing aid. When we spoke to him, he compensated for the hearing deficiency by looking at our lips with a fixed discerning gaze. In form four, we had Mr. Mak, a smooth operator whose lips would become covered with spit as he talked. He left La Salle the following year to start his own profit-oriented school in nearby Kowloon City. We had two teachers in charge of teaching Chinese, Mr. Yip and Mr. Yuen. They maintained a cordial relationship superficially, but when the other wasn't around, they belittled and spoke ill of each other. The science teacher was nicknamed "One-eyed Dragon" because he had a bad eye, and was much feared because of his temper. No one dared misbehave during his class because, with his good eye and bad eye staring in different directions, no one knew who he was looking at.

Form five was a stressful year. That was the year we had to take the city-wide school certificate examination. Our form teacher was Brother Eugene, a bald and intense Irishman with a lisp and a piercing gaze. We had never seen him smile. In marking our English essays, he would award a big zero for the whole paper for a single gross grammatical error. His teaching method, harsh as it might have been, effectively improved our grammar. Having your essay's score and grammatical errors read out aloud in class would make you improve in a hurry.

In years six and seven, we became elite students because the school would take in only fifty or so top students, one group in arts, the other in science. We gathered every morning in a different area from the other students before filing into our classrooms. We even wore a different school tie. All of us were destined for university education. Most of us would settle for Hong Kong University, but some of the math and science geniuses opted for US universities, and would later become professors in some of the top universities in the world.

It was just as competitive in extra-curricular activities, especially in sports. We practiced hard for all sporting events: track and field, swimming, fencing, football, basketball, badminton and table tennis. Being selected for the school teams would be a big deal because one of the Brothers would approach you and invite you to join the team, in front of many admiring classmates. Our best sport was football. Our school team was the best among high schools in the city, having captured the inter-school championship just about every year when I was there. The star footballer was Ip Sheung-wah, nicknamed Darkie for his sun-tanned appearance. He grew up around the playground in Mong Kok. He was good even as a little boy. People would crowd the sidelines of the football pitch whenever he took part in a seven-a-side match, and watched him slide and glide gracefully from one end of the field to the other, controlling the ball as if it were a part of his body, passing adult opponents at will, and scoring with ease. Even the big triad boss in that area was impressed, and summoned him to tell him he would be "protected" in the streets. One time my classmate and I played with him two against one in a mini-game, and we were no match for him even though all three of us were about the same size and age. He was just that much quicker and stronger, and his ball control was so good it seemed that it never left his feet. He was the only La Salle boy I know who later turned professional.

The school also recruited other young crack foot-ballers who would never qualify academically to play for the school team. These boys would fail academi-cally year after year, which was fine with the school because that meant they could stay with the school team for longer.

The school administration seemed to nurture com-petitiveness. For better or worse, that was what elite schools were about. After La Salle, we were much better prepared for the dog-eat-dog world.

In spite of the thuggish reputation, La Salle has not been short of producing stars of the future. Bruce Lee was a La Salle boy. I heard he was expelled because of fighting—no surprise there. His younger brother also studied at La Salle and was one year my junior. He wasn't into fighting, and he looked a lot more Eurasian than Bruce.

Wong Jim was another La Salle boy. He was famous for writing lyrics for some of the most popular songs in Hong Kong, and for being saucy and foul-mouthed in talk shows. He was also indulgent in alcohol, cigarettes, and women in real life. Given that he was head prefect of La Salle in his day, the reputation of La Salle boys was perpetuated generation after generation because of boys like him. Jim died of lung cancer a few years ago, but he had had a rich and colorful life first.

Philip Chan Yan-kin, who was in my class and played soccer with me, was a popular guy in school. He was a ladies' man, and used to throw the parties everyone wanted to go to. He could sing and was in a professional band. His signature song was Del Shannon's *Runaway*.

In a school show, we had all kinds of characters getting on stage to have a rendition of *Runaway* and it was hilarious because, sung off-key, it made people run away.

Philip became a police inspector after La Salle, then later switched careers to become a successful showbiz personality. His last high-profile job was head of a commercial radio station.

Other famous La Salle old boys include my classmates Michael Sze Cho-cheung, Chris Patten's secretary for constitutional affairs, and later CEO of the Trade Development Council; and Jack So Chak-kwong, CEO of the MTR Corporation and other high-profile high-pay jobs. Others include Paul Chow Man-yiu, CEO of Hong Kong Exchanges and Clearing, and Nicholas Ng Wing-fui, secretary for transport in Chris Patten's administration and now chairman of the Public Service Commission.

John Tsang Chun-wah, financial secretary of Donald Tsang's administration, was a La Salle boy.

John Chan Cho-chak, Chairman of the Jockey Club and CEO of the Kowloon Motor Bus Company, and David Tang Wing-cheung, founder of Shanghai Tang and the China Club were students of La Salle, albeit briefly.

Not bad for a school full of thugs.

Fires

MY WIFE LOVES CANDLES. She lights them up for any occasion, including all festivals, visits from friends and family, firework displays in the harbor, and whenever she is in the mood. I am no romantic. I blow out the candles as soon as possible. That's because I am terrified of fires, for good reasons. I had three close encounters with fire in my life.

The last one was minor and it happened recently in our kitchen. My wife left the stove on, boiling a large bone for our newly adopted stray mongrel. She fell asleep in front of the TV in the living room while I slept in the bedroom. I woke up to find a smoke-filled apartment, and a dog licking my face. There were no serious consequences. The kitchen walls were repainted, new fire alarms were installed, and the dog was rewarded with kisses and doggie snacks. It was remarkable in that the dog had been up to then forbidden to enter the master bedroom but had the common sense to breach the rule after having failed to wake my wife in the living room. The incident also underlined my lifelong association with dogs and fires. In the two biggest fires in the history of Hong Kong, I was right there.

The first one was the infamous Shek Kip Mei fire in the Christmas of 1953.

We were living in Sham Shui Po then, on the fourth floor of an old four-story building with no elevator, on Pei Ho Street. To be exact, the five of us—my father, three older sisters and me—lived in one single room in that flat. Four or five other families shared the communal kitchen and bathroom down the corridor. White bedsheets hung from the ceiling served as partitions for privacy. Radio was the main source of entertainment, giving us soap operas involving struggles between young wives and mothers-in-law.

What could make my day would be having a few coins thrown my way so that I could scurry down the stairs and go around the corner to a confectionery store to get a popsicle or some junk food to feed my face. Some days I got doubly lucky. On my way down, the cashier at the Tung Yat Tea House on the first floor would wave me over and tell me to get him a packet of Camel. When I returned with the cigarettes I would always be rewarded with some small change or a pork bun.

The Shek Kip Mei squatter area was right across the street from our building. Kowloon, with the "nine dragons" of hilly geography before widespread reclamations, had little flat land. Most residential slums were built at the foot of a hill, and the Shek Kip Mei squatter area was no exception. Refugees who came earlier chose areas closer to the main road to build their homes. Latecomers lived further and further uphill. From the roof of our building, we could have a panoramic view of the whole settlement. The houses were built from scrap metal and wood, cartons, maybe some bricks and cement, and a lot of tin. Kerosene was the fuel of choice for cooking and illumination.

On that fateful night, fire broke out on one side at around 9:30 at night and it subsided for a while. But soon it rekindled and spread rapidly in all directions because it was Christmas, a time of year with strong seasonal winds.

We were all wide awake up on the rooftop checking on the progress of the fire. The air smelt of burnt wood, and the hillside of Shek Kip Mei lit up like a Christmas tree. I was in a daze because it was way past my bedtime. The last thing I remembered was that my father told us to put on our best clothes, and that we had to go to a friend's house for the night. Why the best clothes? Well, in case everything we owned was burned down, we could at least have what hung on to our bodies.

The worst didn't happen. The fire was controlled around 2:30 in the morning of Christmas Day.

We returned the next day to find our building intact, but the whole squatter area of shanty huts was burnt to the ground and cordoned off. There were people all over the place—policemen, onlookers, and previous residents of the settlement. There were wailing women wanting to go back to the ruins to salvage whatever was left of their possessions, but policemen wouldn't let them. There was a long line of people going around the block, as far away as the Garden factory buildings. (Garden was Hong Kong's major bakery.) The smell of freshly baked bread mixed with that of freshly burnt households. We all went back up to the rooftop, and marveled at what remained of the squatter area, and what could have happened to our building.

That fire, as history has recorded, prompted the Hong Kong government to start a policy of building low-cost public housing for the disadvantaged citizens of the city.

Fires

More than 50,000 people were made homeless as a result of that fire, and the government quickly built twenty-nine blocks of H-shaped seven-story buildings providing utilitarian 120 square-foot flats with communal kitchens and bathrooms to provide housing for the displaced residents of the shanty town. That big residential development was called "resettlement housing estate."

The Shek Kip Mei fire gave birth to the public housing policy of the colonial government. And the rest was history, with unfathomable consequences on the socioeconomic development of Hong Kong for many years to come.

The Shek Kip Mei resettlement houses are still standing today in the same location, albeit dilapidated and empty. The government is talking about keeping and renovating some units as historical monuments.

Another big fire in Hong Kong followed me to Diamond Hill. Diamond Hill and the adjacent villages were full of squatter huts built in the same fashion as in Shek Kip Mei, and kerosene was also used liberally.

It was February of 1964, close to Chinese New Year, and winters were colder and longer in the 60s than today. The dry and windy weather was a perfect recipe for fires to break out and spread. This one started in

Chuk Yuen and quickly spread to Tai Hom Village and Diamond Hill. Although nominally three separate villages, there were no barriers among them, and houses were so close to one another, you could spit out the window and hit your neighbor's outer wall.

There was no panic at all. There was not too much anyone could have in terms of worldly possessions. People stood outside in the open with a few precious belongings and watched the fire's progress. A few were splashing water on their huts as a preventive measure. Children were more excited than fearful. It was past their bedtime and they were excited about being able to stay up so late.

The fire literally stopped at our doorstep. When we were about to flee to a friend's home half a mile away in Sheung Yuen Ling, our front metal door was so close to the fire it was almost too hot to touch. Our neighbor's door, right next to ours, was damaged beyond recognition.

I was quite a bit older than in the Shek Kip Mei fire and during the escape, I offered my sage advice to anyone who would listen: not to bring anything that would make them look stupid, such as a pillow or a broom. I brought along my school books. They were precious to me because I had put in a lot of work in jotting down notes along the margins of the pages.

Fires

As when escaping the Shek Kip Mei fire about ten years earlier, we were told to put on our best clothes. It was close to Chinese New Year, and we dressed up for the festivity prematurely, and showed up at the friend's house at two o'clock in the morning looking ridiculously overdressed.

According to government record, 200 houses were destroyed in that fire and about a thousand people became homeless. Fortunately, no one was injured or killed.

The aftermath was predictable. There was no cordoning off because the involved area was too large and widespread. Looting was not an issue because there was nothing worth looting. There were wailing women claiming to have lost pieces of gold hidden in secret places. We all scoffed at their proclamations.

The recovery was quick. Before long it seemed that all the residences were rebuilt, in the same locations and fashions. Life went on as if nothing had happened. No fanfare, no nonsense, and so Diamond Hill.

The food we ate

I REMEMBER MY YEARS in Diamond Hill as being always hungry. I am not saying I was never fed, just that my craving for food never seemed to cease. I was a growing boy, and unlike in today's households where there are always things in the refrigerator and the kitchen cabinet to munch on, we had food around only during scheduled meals. I was always on the lookout for some extra cash to buy food.

There were many shops down the road which tempted me. For breakfast, they sold congee and *yauh ja gwai,* a fried dough stick which you could split into two long pieces by pulling them apart in the middle. They still sell the thing today, but it is pre-cooked and soggy. Back then it was deep-fried in front of our eyes, and it was quite a spectacle. The cook cut a piece of dough from a large slab, used the back of the knife to make the indentation in the middle, and then stretched it into a thin stick. When put in the large wok with sizzling hot oil, the piece of dough originally the size of a finger would swell up to the size of a forearm and turn brown in a matter of seconds.

The beef starch roll was a new invention. The Cantonese, known to be adventurous in trying out new recipes, used white sticky dough to wrap around ground beef and steamed the combination in a bamboo tray. The same *dim sum* is still available today, in cafés and tea houses, but in addition to beef, shrimps, *char siu* (barbecued pork) and other ingredients are used to fill the roll.

Hot soy milk, scallion pancakes, and pork buns and dumplings were staple breakfast items for the northern Chinese, and they are still around today.

Small restaurants along Diamond Hill road sold the time-honored fast food: *wonton* dumplings, fish balls, and beef brisket noodles. Barbecued meat stalls sold roast pork, barbecued pork, suckling pig, steamed chicken, soy sauce chicken and roast duck. They were made in the same way and looked the same as now, and the taste hasn't changed a bit over the years.

Then there were the itinerant hawkers passing through, peddling stinky tofu, Chinese waffles, beef offal, and barbecued cuttlefish. They all were incredibly tasty to me. But then hunger is the best ingredient for food to taste good.

We also ate a lot of foodstuffs not very popular nowadays. A Cantonese saying went: People can eat any living creature with its back pointing to the sky (that covers just about every living creature except humans). Rice worms, animal blood, water beetles, pig intestines, snakes, frogs, and a myriad of strange vegetables, seaweeds, and mushrooms were readily available.

Rice worms were found among the stalks of grain. They were about the same size and color as a long grain of rice, and were sold by the bucketful. Most of them would be writhing vigorously when placed in a hot wok for stir-frying with salt and pepper. Duck and pig blood were cut into cubes after clotting, and cooked in a soup with radish and fried pork rind. The taste of blood could be best described as metallic, probably because of its iron content.

The water beetle is a flying insect the size and shape of a cockroach. They become pitch black after cooking and the hawker displayed them neatly in layers with their backs facing the sky and heads pointing in the same direction. We peeled the legs and outer skeleton off and ate the rest whole. They tasted salty and juicy. Pig's intestines were loaded with fat appendages, and when put on a frying pan, soon the intestines would be soaked in their own lard. Even I found them hard to swallow.

Snakes were cooked the same way as today. They were skinned and filleted before they were turned into soup. Frogs' hind legs were cooked in the same variety of ways in a restaurant as you would do chicken.

These tastes were easier to develop when young and impressionable. When grown-ups ate something and chewed it loud and fast, the young ones automatically assumed it was tasty. Esthetics aside, all food consists of protein, carbohydrate, and fat, in varying proportions, and mixed in with minerals and water, and perhaps some vitamins. Food was food, and the cheaper the better.

A meal was made of two categories of food: a starch-based item, such as steamed rice or plain noodles which was given the task of filling the stomach and stopping the hunger, and *soong,* which were dishes given the task of adding taste to the rice or noodles, so that they could go down easier. Rice was cheap and *soong* was more expensive. It would be a virtue to eat more rice and less *soong,* so that others at the same dinner table could have a better meal.

We had a lot of vegetables and very little meat on the dinner table. In restaurants, our parents would tell us to order only meat dishes so that we could get our money's worth.

Eggs, including salty duck eggs and century eggs, were also quite affordable, and we had a lot of those. I still remember fondly one egg-and-rice dish in which a raw egg was cracked open and buried in hot steamed rice with dark soy sauce poured over it, followed by hot lard. It was simple but tasty, though not considered healthy by today's standards. We ate a lot of lard, but you looked around and you didn't see any fat people. Food cooked with lard was tasty. Yang Chow fried rice then tasted a lot better than today's dish with the same name because of the lard factor, as did a lot of other dishes.

On special occasions, a whole chicken dish would be served. Preparing the dish started with slaughtering the chicken in the kitchen. After all the blood was drained, the dead bird would be doused with boiling water to facilitate feather plucking. Every part of the chicken except the feathers was food. Chicken feet were mere skin and bones, but the Cantonese had found a way to make them taste good. The dish is still a staple item on the menu of Cantonese restaurants, and is good value for money if one can get over the uneasiness associated with wondering where those feet have been. The rear end of the chicken was actually favored by some people, and is still sold today barbecued in a skewer by street vendors in Taiwan as a delicacy. The offal would be a soup ingredient. The chicken carcass would be served whole, head and all.

The older generation told us that gangsters used to bring out a whole chicken dish to a kidnapped child and watch what he or she went after first to decide how much ransom money to demand. If the kid chose the neck, a large ransom would be asked. If the kid preferred chicken breast, a smaller ransom would be demanded. If the kid went after the leg first, the family was probably dirt poor and the child might as well be set free. In our household, we all preferred the drumstick.

My stepmother's cooking was phenomenal. She would do it only once in a while because she had a full-time job as an inoculation nurse for the Department of Health and she had a low energy level. She was from Sichuan province and hot spicy dishes were supposed to have been invented there. When she cooked, she could cook up a storm. One time she made pork and vegetable dumplings that were so good I had 100 of them. She couldn't make them fast enough for me to wolf down. I actually counted them while I was busy swallowing them one by one, with the whole family cheering me on when I reached number ninety-nine.

My stepmother's other good dishes were pork chops and chili prawns. The process of making them was so elaborate that it would have made preparing for a heart transplant operation look simple. I learned how to make them watching from the sidelines and I am still getting kudos whenever I serve them to my guests today. My stepmother made spicy dishes, but funnily enough, although from Sichuan, she couldn't handle hot food while everyone else in the household could.

Food prepared by our amah Ah Ho was bland and was either over- or under-cooked. Preparing food for us was not her priority because she was often preoccupied with gambling. My wake-up call was usually her scraping the charred surface of our toast with a knife.

In summer, we often had comfort food: fried rice noodles with bean sprouts and red bean soup for dessert. The dessert was so sweet because there was so much brown sugar put in it that it would make our teeth tinkle. We also made grass jelly with syrup poured over it. To lower the temperature for the jelly to gel we had to buy a block of ice sold by a vendor pushing a large cart up and down Diamond Hill Road. The refrigerator was an unknown household item. We also had other home-made desserts. A millstone was used to crush and pulverize peanuts or sesame seeds. It was operated by hand and worked by rotating an upper heavier part on a lower stand, trapping and grinding the kernels in the middle. Adding water to a small aperture at the top of the millstone made the rotating smoother and easier. After boiling the peanut or sesame paste with brown sugar, the final products were the famous peanut and sesame sweet soups. They are still available in restaurants today, but no doubt they come in cans and are not home-made.

In winter, our comfort food was hot pot with charcoal burnt in a special cooking utensil. Everything tasted good when piping hot.

We seldom ate out, and if we did, there was coaching from the parents as to what to order and how to behave. Going to a tea house for *dim sum* was usually on a Sunday around noon, and it was quite an ordeal because every other family seemed to have the same agenda and scrambling for an open table could take hours. The usual practice, uncouth as it might have been, was to stand and wait beside some strangers' table and stare at them eating until they called for the tab and quit.

My father took us to Western restaurants once in a long while, to teach us Western table manners and the proper way to use European cutlery. All that effort was wasted on me because as soon as I set foot on American soil years later, I found out that American people ate a lot of dishes with their fingers, and preferred using the fork instead of the knife for cutting up food.

My father was an educated man who received part of his education in North Carolina in the US, and he was very much into table manners. Elbows on the table, talking with a mouthful of food, and spitting unwanted food directly onto the table or the floor were banned around our dinner table. I thought at that time he was prudish, and was taking the fun out of eating.

That's why I enjoyed eating at *dai pai dong*s where he was never around. *Dai pai dong*s were all alfresco affairs, and there were two types of seating: regular tables and chairs, and high stools adjacent to the cooking area. On top of the high stools were small stools for customers to squat on. Many grassroots people enjoyed eating in a squatting position, and it was also more natural and entertaining to spit unwanted food onto the ground from that height.

Food being such an important part of Chinese culture and existence, what we ate reflected how much money we earned. The poorest families often had vegetable and salty fish for dinner, and the saying "vegetable and salty fish" became a curse and a lexicon to describe a downtrodden situation. But during festivals, even the poorest families would have something extra on the dinner table—rice dumplings during Dragon Boat, mooncake, star fruit and pomelo for dessert during Mid-Autumn, and multiple dishes with auspicious names and sweets during Chinese New Year.

Tough as our life was, our countrymen back in the Mainland had it even tougher at that time. My stepmother sent back home every month cans of lard mixed with chili pepper and dried shrimps, which her sisters and brothers could mix with brown rice and feed their families day after day.

Growing up in Diamond Hill among Cantonese neighbors taught me a lot about their food folklore. For instance, the Cantonese had a name for an all-encompassing and nebulous condition with symptoms that ranged from halitosis and constipation to acne and coughing—*yeh hei* (literally "hot air.") The remedy would be an herbal concoction known as "cool tea"—the ultimate *yin-yang* theory of disease and cure. Abstinence from fried food was also recommended as part of the remedy. Such dietary advice epitomizes Chinese folklore in being short on science, but long on pragmatism. It has never been proven that fried food can cause *yeh hei,* but it really doesn't matter—eating less fried food is good for your health regardless.

Traditional Chinese medicine has always been intertwined with folklore. When I was living in Diamond Hill, people dealt with many medical problems based on older people's opinions and not professional advice. Western doctors were not trusted and they were also too expensive. The Cantonese gave new meaning to the saying: You are what you eat. The conventional wisdom was that eating certain kinds of food and abstinence from others determined your well-being. Many believed that whichever part of your body was weak or sick, you could build strength of that part by eating the corresponding part from animals. For example, if you sprained your ankle, you should eat chicken feet for a week. If you thought you had kidney disease, you should consume pig's kidney regularly.

The urine of a young virgin boy was also very much sought after by a few ignorant men. We only learnt of it when we witnessed a screaming young mother chasing after a man who had just collected a cupful of urine from her young son while urinating in the street and had gulped it down quickly.

Maybe a bit on the ridiculous side was the belief by some men that consuming male reproductive organs from animals perceived to be virile, such as rhinos, tigers, and bears, which were much sought after as aphrodisiacs, could improve their own sexual prowess. Snakes could do the job as well, and they were a lot cheaper. In Temple Street, you could find daring young men biting the heads off snakes for show to attract customers. And then they drained snake blood into beer for the young men lining up to chug-a-lug before swaggering off next door to a bordello.

The games we played

BEING POOR DOES NOT NECESSARILY mean being deprived of fun. I had lots of fun growing up, even though I don't remember my parents ever bringing home any toys for me. I managed to create fun playing with things that were free or dirt cheap.

For example, we collected and played with bottle caps. We flicked them with the middle finger and they traveled far on a smooth surface. We lined them up on the floor, and whoever could knock the most from the line from a distance by flicking a "cue cap" across the room won the game. Alternatively, we hammered the cap flat, punched two holes in the center with a nail, passed a string through the holes, and we had a spinning toy operated by pulling the string and relaxing it. We also sharpened the edges of the flattened cap by grinding them on a rough surface, and then the spinning toy became a weapon we used to cut things and to terrorize family members.

Boys being boys, we were into weapons. I made use of my father's discarded razors, attaching them to clothespins held in place by rubber bands. I kept a cache of such weapons in the mini-attic between the kitchen and the bathroom. They were there for me to look at and have, even though using them for fighting never crossed my mind. I did use them to carve my name all over the place, but not much else.

Bottle caps and discarded razors were free, and there were some cheap Chinese toys available. There were the top, the hacky sack, and rattles and toy weapons made out of bamboo and rattan. There were handicraft figurines and simple mind games. But by the time we lived in Diamond Hill, I had passed the age of playing with most of them.

I would love to have owned a bicycle, but it would have attracted burglary. And if ridden in a thorough-fare, the chances of being hit by a car were there. At least those were my father's reasons, and that was the end of it.

We were into fads and susceptible to Western influences, but only if the plaything was affordable. The yo-yo and the hula hoop belong to this category and they came and went in a flash.

The yo-yo craze was started by an American soft drink company. You collected enough of their bottle caps, and you would be rewarded with a designer yo-yo. Going up and down was for amateurs. There were tricks shown in the instruction brochure that came with my new yo-yo with names like "rocking the cradle" and "walking the dog."

The hula hoop was promoted through TV, which showed young ladies gyrating their hips to upbeat music. The game was probably designed for women, because my sisters picked up the thing for the first time and it would stay around their waists and off the ground for hours, while I could never master that thing, which kept sliding down to my ankles no matter how hard I tried. It was probably a good thing. I didn't think too many people would be interested in watching my hips gyrate.

During the Chinese New Year, we played with firecrackers. We didn't just light up once and leave a whole string of them to explode, making a whole lot of noise and nothing else. We lit the crackers one by one, so that they could last longer. If you put an empty tin can over a lit cracker, the tin would blast straight up into the sky real high, and come straight down, spectacularly. The timing had to be right, if you covered it too soon, oxygen might run out and it died. If too late, your finger might get blown off. That was the idea—to live dangerously. There were also the usual teenage boys' pranks of scaring girls when they least expected, such as in the toilet or around the corner.

In later years, in addition to conventional firecrackers, more sophisticated gunpowder-based products which could make noise, explode, sparkle in the dark, and travel far in a trajectory were available. In retrospect, these "toys" were dangerous and children shouldn't be allowed to touch them. My fingers got burned quite a few times. Luckily, nothing more serious happened.

The colonial government banned firecrackers in the late 60s because of the large number of injuries during Chinese New Year, especially to the eyes. The ban was mostly enforced in urban areas. Indigenous inhabitants of the New Territories, because of the lawlessness in their culture, especially in matters hard to enforce, have continued with the custom up to today.

I liked games that were competitive and involved some stakes. When we played with marbles, the better player would end up owning more marbles than they started out with. We played on dirt and we used a sharp object to make a circle at one end and a straight line about ten feet away. Every player chipped in one or two marbles to put inside the circle, and threw a cue marble towards the line. Whoever's cue marble was closest to the line could start the game. First you tried to get your cue marble close to the circle and on your next shot, you tried to knock the marbles out of the circle with your cue marble and whatever marbles you knocked out you could keep. The trick was for your cue marble to stay out of the circle, or else there would be a one-marble penalty, returned to the circle at your expense. We learned to put spins on the cue marble to draw it back after striking to avoid the penalty. You continued to play if you scored, and if you cleared all the marbles in the circle in one go, all other players had to pay you double. When you played with younger and lesser players, you didn't want to do that too often—they simply wouldn't play with you anymore. So you missed on purpose once in a while. I picked on younger players and won most days. My pastime at home during that fad was to count my marbles, literally.

When sent out on chores, I would stop by the roadside for a game or two before returning home, and would outsmart my father by washing the dirt off my knuckles before I got home.

Another fad around the same time was collecting and playing with cards printed with famous historical and fictional characters from comic books, equivalent to baseball cards in America. Each player chipped in a few cards, and after having decided who would go first with paper, scissors, and stone, each player took a turn to flip and keep as many cards as he could by clapping once in front of the stack of cards. I did well in that game too, and soon earned the nickname Big Hands.

If only I had kept those cards, I could be a rich man now, auctioning them off to rich Hong Kong men who might want to buy back some memories.

There was a special place in my heart for kite-flying. Even today, when I see a kite up in the sky, my heart skips a beat. I liked the colors and designs on kites, and nothing could make my day like a brightly colored kite up in the air against a clear blue sky, and the sun so bright it traced the white thread all the way from the reel to the kite a thousand feet or more high. But simply flying the kite wasn't our game. We didn't play nice. The game was about who could cut other people's kites loose by severing their threads with yours.

I manufactured my own killer thread so that it could be cheaper and meaner. First I broke a glass bottle, collected all the broken pieces into a tin can, and used a long piece of rock to create my own pestle and mortar to smash and grind the glass into powder.

I then passed some strong thick thread through another tin can filled with glue followed by the tin can with the powdered glass. The thread was then left to dry before being wound up onto a rattan reel.

There was nothing like navigating your kite to sweep across another kite's path and using those sharp serrated edges on your thread to cut loose someone else's kite, and watching other boys run and scramble after it to claim ownership.

On a few occasions, I ruled the sky by cutting loose all the kites in sight, in the presence of several adoring younger boys. Finding no other kites to terrorize, I would reel my kite in before I swaggered off home, face flushed and heart pounding. There and then, I knew how Genghis Khan must have felt after winning a battle.

Flying kites was not half as brutal as another game we played, using small insects we called "crabs." In playing that game, the only stake was the insects' lives. They didn't cost anything and they were low maintenance creatures. Throwing in a dead fly every other day would keep them alive for weeks at least. They looked like miniature crabs, with numerous legs and a round body. They were not crickets because they didn't make noises and not spiders because they didn't make webs. There were a variety of them, all sharing the same penchant for fighting. The common ones were gray in color, but they were no match for special species like the dark "old jabber" with its pair of long front legs, and the "red kid" with its bright red and stout body. These insects could be captured between thorny leaves of shrubs found all over the hills. I learned how to make cages to house these insects out of the thorny leaves using my cache of razor weapons. They were also easy to handle. With the gate of the cage ajar and a finger there, they would jump onto the finger to be carried to another cage to fight its own kind.

The fight was usually swift with the two insects charging towards and then head-butting each other like bulls. It usually didn't take long for one to back off and scoot away. But that wasn't enough for us; we were not normal kids. When we got bored, we trapped the two insects in the same closed cage, to open it an hour or so later, usually to find one insect having been the other's dinner.

We played with all kinds of insects. There was a fable about a little boy whose family couldn't afford the oil that could be used in a lamp for him to study at night, so he collected fireflies in a cloth bag. Because of the fireflies, he was able to make it big in the national examination, and subsequently became a mandarin, and brought honor to his whole family. We had fireflies in summer and autumn in Diamond Hill, and yours truly trapped a bunch of them in a bag and guess what, there was no light coming out from that bag because the bugs died quickly under such circumstances, and dead bugs don't shine.

We also had lots of dragonflies around. I caught one and tied a piece of thread around the poor bugger's waist and wondered if I could fly it like a kite. I was imagining all the possibilities. Well, it didn't work half as well as I imagined. The dragonfly became halved.

The games we played when we were kids in Diamond Hill hardly cost anything but they were fun. Unlike computer games kids play nowadays, they required a certain amount of creativity, ingenuity, and people skill. No batteries required, either.

When I was fourteen or fifteen years old, I was almost as tall as my father and had outgrown all those children's games. Instead, I started to do sports.

Table tennis was my first sport. I beat my older sisters playing on our dinner table, and made them cry.

The problem with playing table tennis was that you needed a table to play on and there was a dearth of tables around. We ended up playing on any flat surface, with a long object put across in the middle to serve as the net, and using thin hardback books as paddles. And that was no fun.

The Catholic church around the corner had a real table. At one time, I spent a lot of time there—in the table tennis room, not the church proper. I played there until I was thrown out of that church because they found out I never attended their catechism classes.

Even though we had tennis courts in La Salle College, they were off limits to us. Another problem with playing tennis was that new balls were required once in a while, and they were expensive. I had a distant cousin who lived in a big house with a garden in Kowloon Tong. His father was a wealthy garment factory owner. He played tennis in La Salle College because he was in the school team, and he practiced and took lessons in the Kowloon Tong Club. There was no way I could afford any of those things.

My enthusiasm for table tennis was soon overtaken by soccer, which you could play just about anywhere. You could entertain yourself for hours by kicking the ball against a wall or up into the air repeatedly and not allowing it to touch the ground to practice ball control. As soon as you could find an empty lot and kicked a ball around for a while, a number of boys would gather around you. You then put in place two objects, such as school bags, serving as goal posts, and voilà! You could start a match.

I used to play a lot of soccer. In the summer months when there was no school, I would wake up at seven o'clock and run to the football field miles away, play until noon, run back home to have lunch, and run back out to continue the game until dark. When there were too many people in the field, we divided ourselves into teams, and would take turns playing, twenty minutes for each session, with the victorious team staying on.

The matches were played in a surprisingly friendly atmosphere, considering the large number of thugs in the area. But soccer, like all other games we played in Diamond Hill, followed a hierarchical system. Boys of similar ages played together, and grown men had their own teams.

Football was by far the most popular sport then. It belonged to the hoi polloi. Tennis, cricket, hockey, softball, volleyball, and badminton were elite sports that required special facilities. They were played in institutions and private clubs.

We also played a little basketball, convinced that it would make us grow taller. There was only one basketball court in the neighborhood, which was often used for playing soccer instead. In retrospect, we often violated the rules of the game, since none of us had ever seen a real basketball match. For instance, many of us ran with the ball without dribbling or when we dribbled we put both hands on the ball.

One day I showed my friends how I could grab the basketball with one hand, and they said: "We didn't call you Big Hands for nothing." That re-affirmed my nickname, which I got stuck with for years to come.

One life-long habit I developed as a result of play-ing football was drinking beer. Umbrella introduced beer to me one day, telling me that a beer from China called Tsingtao was actually cheaper than Coca Cola, the predominant soft drink then, and the bottle was twice as big. A big bottle of beer after football on a hot day was like heaven on earth. They sold beer to juveniles in Diamond Hill. We even drank it in front of the storekeepers. But no worries, the beer drinking never got out of hand, not because of my mental fortitude, but because of my cash flow problem. Being poor had its advantages.

Gambling

OUR AMAH AH HO was from Shun Tak, a village in Guangdong province famous for good home-style cooking, wealthy people, and a sect of women sworn to celibacy. Ah Ho was none of those. Already in her 50s when she started working for us, she was sworn to, if anything, playing mahjong.

On my way home after school every afternoon, I would be greeted by the sight of an older woman with gray hair tied in a bun, a slightly hunched back, and reading glasses perched on her nose, sitting at a mahjong table in the front of a shop close to home.

She worked for a household of seven people, had to do laundry by hand, prepare three meals a day, wash dishes after each one, and clean house, and yet she could find time to play mahjong just about every afternoon. Naturally, the quality of her work left much to be desired, but my parents were very tolerant of her.

There was no question of her loyalty. One time while I was playing a coin game in the square down Diamond Hill Road, I saw Ah Ho, in her trademark plain *cheongsam* top and black baggy pants, running frantically uphill toward home and turning her head back frequently to look, as if she was being pursued by an assassin. When I returned home, I asked my sisters what that was about. It turned out my father had needed a taxi—a rare occasion—and Ah Ho went down to the entrance of Diamond Hill Road to hail one, and instead of using it to get home, she led the driver home by running in front of it to save my father money.

Her pay was thirty dollars a month when she first started, when my father's monthly pay was about 600. It was very little money even for that epoch, but it was the going rate. She could only afford playing mahjong for small change. Her partners-in-crime were young housewives half her age and men even younger, all with more or less the same disposable income. They set up tables in shop fronts, and Ah Ho usually played there until six in the evening, right before my parents came home from work. She then rushed to the wet market to buy groceries, and had dinner ready by seven. When she was in a losing streak, we would find more or less the same dishes on the table for a whole week. When she was winning, we would find a surprise treat such as barbecue pork from the restaurant in the market.

Ah Ho was illiterate, and I had to write letters on her behalf to her relatives back in Shun Tak, but she knew the characters on the mahjong tiles well. She could rub her thumb on the surface of the tiles and tell them apart without looking at them—a useful skill if you play in public and you don't want kibitzers behind you to know your hand. She was a skillful player, and could hold her own against anyone in spite of her age and education level. Given that mahjong was her only entertainment and that she was doing it within her means, she was not causing any problem for anyone.

Her son-in-law, however, was a problem gambler and the curse of her family. He was a barber, and spent all his earnings on supporting his gambling habits. He lived apart from Ah Ho's daughter, only to return for a free meal and an opportunity to knock her up. She ended up rearing five children by him on her own by taking up numerous odd jobs, even when she was under treatment for tuberculosis. Ah Ho helped her out by having two of her children live with her on and off in our household.

It seemed that most barbers were problem gamblers. They gambled with cards in between customers, and stayed behind to play mahjong after closing the shop. On horse-racing days, the radio would be broadcasting the races live. God forbid if your barber was listening to the announcement in the middle of cutting your hair and his horse didn't come in, he could get so frustrated he took it out on your head with a pair of scissors.

There were many other problem gamblers around. The twin brothers who lived nearby would be scared to death every time their father returned home in a bad mood because of gambling losses. They were severely beaten once because of something that involved wasting ten cents, when the father could be gambling away hundreds of dollars regularly.

A friend of my parents worked as a supporting actor in movies. He was always broke but couldn't live without playing mahjong. As is usually the case, the desperate one always loses. He borrowed from everyone, and lost first his dignity, then his life by drowning himself in a well.

Pawn shops took in mundane stuff like a blanket or old clothing. We heard quarrels between husbands and wives, and between friends about needing this blanket or that heavy coat because the weather had turned cold.

My parents also liked playing mahjong. They played it with friends every weekend. I didn't mind that at all, because it meant I could watch mahjong all day and had better food for dinner. My father had three regular mahjong partners, all well-educated non-Cantonese refugees. Sometimes they played all through the night. We knew it would be an all-nighter when they put a blanket on top of the mahjong table to reduce the noise level. One of them was a sore loser, and when it was time to count the winnings and losses the next morning, he, unshaven and disheartened, would moan and groan as if it was the end of the world.

Mr. Lin was a regular, until he died suddenly of liver cancer at a relatively young age. He was replaced by a Mr. Tam, who was a heavy smoker. I purchased cigarettes for him when he ran out, and got my usual commission. Mr. Wong, another regular, died of liver cancer, too, a few years later. My father had to expand his circle of mahjong friends to include husbands of my stepmother's friends.

My stepmother had her own circle, all from her home town in Sichuan. Her regular partners were Mrs. Yang, Mrs. Loh, and Mrs. Pang. Mrs. Pang later became Mrs. Hsu, because, according to my step-mother, Mrs. Pang dumped Mr. Pang to marry Dr. Hsu for money, who was forced to divorce his wife, even after she attempted suicide. The former Mrs. Pang blushed furiously when my stepmother made us greet her as Mrs. Hsu instead of Mrs. Pang. It was all soap opera material.

We learned mahjong at an early age. I had my first taste of the game at the age of nine, when I was barely literate.

Gambling became rampant around Chinese New Year when everyone would have some money and such behavior was condoned, even with children. It was customary for men to gamble and women to prepare food all night long on Chinese New Year's eve. Gambling continued until maybe the tenth of the lunar month when *lai see* had dried up. By our early teens, my friends and I had already mastered all the common gambling games: mahjong, poker, Russian poker, *fan-tan, pai kau, tin kau,* Big and Small, Three Kings, blackjack, and so on.

For the rest of the year, we kids wouldn't have enough money for serious gambling, but I could always "find" some loose change in my father's suit pockets to do some minor gambling, such as a coin game we played on dirt. We hit a coin against a flat surface on a slant so that the coin would roll away. Whoever had the farthest coin could start first. We chased after each other's coins, and if you could hit someone else's coin with yours by aiming and throwing at it, you owned it. The game required the skills of a sharpshooter. How did I fare in this game? I'll put it this way—that was how I found out I needed glasses.

We gambled on anything; even a high-brow game like Chinese chess was reduced to the lowest denominator of ten cents a game. We gave new meaning to the Chinese saying: "you can find treasure in a book," because when no other gambling tool was available or allowable (for instance, in a classroom), we gambled by flipping a book and using the page number as a card surrogate in a perverted version of blackjack.

There were no age barriers when it came to gambling in Diamond Hill. We used to play Russian poker with a seventy-year-old man in Tai Lin's place. He had a stroke a few years back and couldn't shuffle or deal cards, so it was up to us, the younger generation, to do the honor. I had a friend named Pui Chuen, who was a straight-A student and was good at everything he did, including all kinds of gambling. We were not in Pui Chuen's league, so we gambled with his younger brother, a nine-year-old who kicked our butts every time.

Being good at gambling could be a curse. Both Pui Chuen and his brother were talented, but both quit school early. Pui Chuen found out that easy money could be made from gambling and snooker hustling, so he lost interest in school after form three. He played truant for a few years, wandering from the mahjong table to the billiards parlor, mixing up day and night.

He was the reason I got interested in snooker and billiards. He took me to a parlor in Jordan, the basement of a theater-cum-shopping center complex called Po Hing. I got hooked even though I was never as good as he was. Thank God for that, otherwise I would have had a misspent youth like his. Snooker parlors had a reputation of seediness, full of gangsters and hustlers. That was about right. It was not the kind of place parents wanted their sons to spend time in. But snooker was a perfect game for the Chinese in many ways. It didn't require great physical strength; it was played in a smoke-filled room; and it involved gambling.

The best snooker player in Hong Kong then was a guy nicknamed Four-eyed Tam. He wore black-rimmed glasses, and when he aimed, you could see the hair hanging on his forehead vibrate. The number-two player was "Bank-shot" Wah, from his uncanny ability to make bank shots from all angles. Tse Yin was a regular. He was a big-shot movie star then, a lot bigger than his son Nicholas Tse, today's Canto star, whose claim to fame so far has not been acting or singing, but getting involved in traffic accidents. Tse Yin could control the speed of the cue ball such that it would stop at any designated spot. His nickname was Lig Sui, which means exact speed.

The best billiards player was a businessman nick-named Billiard King Yu. In billiards, you can score by hitting the red ball with your own white cue ball and make the cue ball go into a pocket. He could play like a machine, scoring point after point by the same shot, with the object red ball ending up in the same spot after each shot over and over again. We used to sit around and watch him play, scoring points in the hundreds.

Then there were the myriad of hustlers around. Pui Chuen was one of them. The trick in snooker hustling is to make your victim feel he has a chance. So, you always try to win by a small margin. Pui Chuen taught me when to quit, and who to avoid.

There was this short unassuming guy who had a hunched back and the worst possible form in snooker. He used a cue stick that was dirty and old, but he was the most successful hustler in the snooker parlor. Whenever he got himself a sucker, we all gathered around to watch with glee. The hunchback always consoled his victims by blaming bad luck for their losses. They kept coming back.

The reason I didn't get sucked into a life like Pui Chuen's was not because of my mental fortitude, but my lack of money. Pui Chuen seemed to have unlimited cash, thanks to his gambling successes and his parents' permissiveness. On the other hand, my father gave me not much pocket money, but plenty of lectures on the importance of a good education.

Pui Chuen saw things my father's way in his late twenties when he fell in love, had plans for marriage, and realized the opportunities lost. He tried to make up for lost time by quitting gambling and enrolling in evening classes. In spite of his talents, he was forever condemned to mediocrity because although he won in gambling he had lost the best years of his life because of it.

The Jockey Club was the only organization allowed by law to conduct any gambling activities. Apart from horse racing, the club also had a weekly lottery ticket called Ma Bill (horse-racing note). The ticket looked like paper money with a watermark picture of race horses and a serial number printed at the bottom.

Each cost one dollar, and with the winning number you could receive up to one million dollars in prize money. A mahjong friend of my parents became wealthy all of a sudden, and he claimed to have mobilized his enormous wealth from the Mainland. But since nobody had ever heard of his wealth in his former life, the court of rumor decreed that this mediocre man made it big on account of hitting the jackpot in Ma Bill.

There was also an illegal lottery run by shady characters in the neighborhood. It was called Chi Fa (flower numbers). It appealed to people such as Ah Ho and other poorer inhabitants of Diamond Hill because it would cost only ten cents to play. You picked a number, from one to fifty, and you got a handwritten receipt on a piece of crap paper. At four o'clock in the afternoon, a number would be announced through the grapevine. No one knew or cared how that number was decided. I told Ah Ho repeatedly it could be a sham, but spending ten cents to spring for hope was enough of an allure for Ah Ho.

All gamblers are superstitious, to some degree. We learned from elders and also from experience not to do certain things when gambling. For example, we were not supposed to touch anyone's shoulders, or show or touch anyone with a book, which in Cantonese sounds exactly like losing. There were so many taboos you might as well not be there. I used to stand behind my father watching him play mahjong, and there were good days and bad days. When my father had a string of lucky hands, I would get a small reward from him at the end of the game for bringing him good luck. On his bad days, he looked at me funny and would get me off his back as quickly as possible by sending me away with a coin or two. I was like a fund manager, I made money no matter which way the market went.

I had the most mind-boggling and life-altering experience while watching Ah Ho play mahjong, and it had nothing to do with superstition. One of her partners was a young housewife from a nearby village. She had her four-year-old son with her. It was not unusual for mothers to bring children to a mahjong game. It was fascinating to witness a mother carrying one child on her back in a cloth strap, breast-feeding another one, and screaming at the eldest for running around, all the while playing mahjong and winning. This four-year-old boy wasn't running around. He was sitting at a table quietly by himself and playing with cards. He was shuffling and dealing the cards like a pro. I was maybe fourteen or fifteen then and was quite full of myself. Ah Ho yelled over to me that this boy was smart. She had no idea. I went over and asked the boy what he was doing, and he said he was trying to figure out which cards were face up and which ones down. I said that would be too easy. The card with the face up we could see what it was. But that was for you and me. For him, all the cards, face up or down, were in plain view. I was in shock. I was studying physics, chemistry and biology, and at that level, everything was black and white. What I had in front of my eyes was supernatural, and could not be explained by logic as I had known it. I was skeptical and asked permission to take the boy back to my home close by to play. I used my own deck of cards and after some vigorous shuffling, put a few random cards face down, and that boy could identify all of them each and every time. I was really excited and tried to summon my sisters to show them. They didn't want to be bothered; probably because I had exhausted my cry-wolf quota. They didn't know what they had missed.

That was the first and last time I saw that boy. I sure would like to meet him again today, to see if he still has that power. From what I read, people with ESP tend to lose it with advancing age, before they would be old enough to be allowed in a casino. Nature has a

way of playing tricks with talented people and equaliz-
ing all of us sooner or later.

The encounter with that boy had affected me in a
positive way. I began to realize that I did not know
everything, and I should keep an open mind. Years
later, many people called me an old soul before I was
close to being old. Ever since that day, I have always
tried to give everyone and every situation the benefit
of the doubt.

Now that I am older, I have become interested in
the afterlife and I did a lot of reading on it, and other
psychic studies that are not considered mainstream
science but are actually quite logical and intelligent if
you open your mind to them. There are people among
us who have ESP and can see things the rest of us can't,
although they are the minority and are easily dis-
missed as con men or freaks. By the same token, it is
quite possible that there can be apparitions, hauntings,
poltergeists, near-death experiences, out-of-body
experiences, and *feng shui.* I am particularly interested
in afterlife because this life has been so nice and
enjoyable I want an extension of it. I wouldn't go as
far as some psychical researchers who are quoted as
saying they couldn't wait to die to find out what would
happen in the next life. I would like to live this life to
the fullest until the time comes for me to find out

what happens next. I sure don't want to gamble this one away.

In Diamond Hill, most gambling occurred in households, but for high rollers, there were illegal gambling dens, run by men with triad connections. They were intimidating places not meant for the faint-hearted. I was not brave enough to mingle with the high rollers, but Umbrella took me there just to watch. There were guards at the entrance and the inside of the establishment was windowless and rustic. The amount of money on the games table was breath-taking. My fearless friend Umbrella occasionally placed bets, and if the amount was deemed too minuscule by their standards, the croupier would give him a look that could kill. Regular customers wore gold Rolexes and lots of gold jewelry. The gold could be used as collateral when they ran out of money.

I started to get into the act in gambling dens in my late teens when I had paper money instead of just coins. Blackjack was the most popular game then, and one of the regulars was a movie star by the name of Tso Tat-wah. In movies, he played either a police detective or a *kung fu* master. In real life, he played the fool. He made hundreds of movies and at one time owned a movie studio and half a block of properties somewhere in Kowloon. He, however, was cursed by the gambling bug. Legend had it he lost his studio in an overnight poker game. He then lost all his properties one by one until his wife begged him to hold on to the last one where they lived.

He used to coach us young amateurs how to play blackjack, when to draw and when to hold, but we would do exactly the opposite, knowing that he was the biggest loser of all time. He died in 2007. Years before his death, he had been dead broke and had lived off handouts from friends.

There were also mahjong parlors where you could go by yourself and play with strangers. They were tough and rough places, frequented by ruffians and seasoned gamblers. Difficult customers, especially those who were slow to pay up, would be taken outside by the bouncers and taught a lesson. They had a set of rules different from those of household mahjong. Many of the rules were there to prevent cheating. The customary penalty was, quite fittingly, to have the knuckles of the cheating hand smashed by a hammer. Umbrella witnessed such a punishment once. He told me they were "kind enough" to allow the cheating woman to bite down hard on her own slippers when the hammer came down.

I grew up in Diamond Hill thinking everybody gambled, more or less. There were exceptions, of course, like our next-door neighbor Mr. Perfect, the father of Chubby and Skinny. Ah Ho's grandchildren never gambled (their father did enough of that for all of them), including her only grandson Ah Fai, who later became a successful ophthalmologist in Taiwan.

Ah Ho worked for my parents and played mahjong until she was diagnosed to have colon cancer in her early seventies. She died soon after. Her son-in-law, in his old age, lived with the family. The ultimate punishment for him came during family gatherings in those later years when all his children had good jobs and successful marriages, but he had nothing to show. He died not too long ago, in shame no doubt.

Drinking is the curse of the Irish; gambling the curse of the Chinese. When I was living in New York City, I was a regular in an Irish pub in Lower Manhattan. One night, some customers started a coin guessing game, and asked me if I would like to join in. The bartender said: "Of course he will. All Chinese gamble." My response to that was: "This one also drinks."

Thugs and gangsters

THERE WERE THREE MAJOR "TRIBES" in Diamond Hill. The biggest was the Cantonese, mainly indigenous Hong Kong people or refugees from Guangdong province. The Chiu Chow refugees were a force to be reckoned with. And the rest were all called Shanghainese. The Cantonese had this habit of calling anyone who spoke any non-Cantonese dialect a Shanghainese.

My father's ancestors originated from Zhejiang, and he was born and raised in Xian and Wuhan. He spoke Cantonese with a heavy accent, and he was immediately labeled a Shanghainese.

There is safety in numbers. The Cantonese produced the largest number of thugs and triad members. They also looked down on anyone who spoke with an accent.

The Chiu Chow people could hold their own because they had a reputation for being fierce fighters and being loyal to their own people. One of their favorite sayings was: *Gaa gie noun,* which means *paisan* in mafia-speak. When a fight broke out between a Chiu Chow group and another group, you could count on other Chiu Chow people in the area to join in. Chiu Chow people fought among themselves, too; but all would be forgotten when outside people were involved.

The "Shanghainese" were generally meek people. Most of them were not literally Shanghainese anyway, and could have been from any province other than Guangdong. There was no bond among them. Genuine Shanghainese, rightly or wrongly, had a reputation for being wily and having a penchant for pretending to be richer than they really were. They were also formidable businessmen.

My mother was from Chiu Chow, my father was Shanghainese, and I spoke perfect Cantonese. So I'd be whatever worked to my advantage. Among Chiu Chow people, I'd be *gaa gie noun,* I spoke Mandarin with the Shanghainese, and among Cantonese, no one had to know I wasn't one of them.

In spite of my father's worries, I could never become a thug or a triad member, because I was a coward and I was not cruel enough. I did not grow up in a family full of thugs. Also, even at a young age,

I believed I would have a future. There was nothing in my formative years that was conducive to a life of crime.

Ah Noun, on the other hand, was spoiled rotten by his mother. The "uncles" who visited him once in a while were macho guys who promised him protection and taught him life lessons not in what not to do, but how not to get caught doing what should not be done. He was hopeless in school, and was a natural-born fighter. When he was seventeen, he fought with another thug in a nearby village over a girl, and got stabbed in the abdomen. After leaving hospital, he had to marry the girl because she was pregnant. He took up a job as a marine policeman later, and told us not to call him Ah Noun but call him Double Eight, his badge number. His mother made his wife wash his feet every day when he came home from work or else she would be beaten. I witnessed the beatings with my own eyes, and they were brutal. What was memorable to me was not only the face of a young woman smeared with blood and tears but also the expression of nonchalance on the face of Ah Noun, as if it was none of his business.

Ah Noun got into trouble when he abandoned mother, wife, and son and everyone else and started going to "dance halls," where men paid to dance and chat with young women. He borrowed heavily and ran afoul of the law to earn desperate cash. All this happened before he turned twenty. He spent the rest of his life in jail or running.

Ah Noun's cousin was a thug of a different kind. His nickname was "Bull." He looked like one and behaved even worse. He was an epileptic, and did not receive the best of medical care. His fits must have deprived him of oxygen to his brain, because he was borderline retarded. His father, who was a well-respected member of the Chiu Chow fraternity, always insisted it was karma and not illness that had caused his son's problems. You should have seen the father's face whenever Bull was lying on the ground convulsing. It seemed the father was suffering more pain and despair than the son.

It didn't help to have a cousin like Ah Noun, who frequently led him astray by getting him in all sorts of trouble. Ah Noun would taunt him into getting into fights with people just for kicks. To get his own kicks, Bull went around sexually assaulting young girls. He approached the victim from the opposite direction and swung his hand towards her crotch and squeezed it so hard the girl screamed and sometimes passed out in pain.

One of the victims was my friend's sister. The family was so traumatized they didn't talk to anyone in the neighborhood for years.

Another thug I knew had a worse childhood. Ah Noun and Bull were violent and dumb. This one was violent and psychotic. His nickname was Kwai Tsai (ghost boy) because he had light blond hair, blue eyes, and freckles on his face. He had always been an angry young man, for good reasons. His Chinese mother worked in a Wan Chai bar, and it was common knowledge what she did for a living, and the other kids wouldn't let him forget it. He was much feared because he used weapons when he fought. He would produce a knife or an axe at the slightest provocation. Policemen were usually called. One time I saw a tall plain-clothed policeman take his axe from him by a *kung fu* move that would do Bruce Lee proud. I was so impressed that I tried to talk my father into giving me money for *kung fu* lessons. I did not get it. Whenever I asked for anything, my father would lecture me on the power of the pen. That's why I am torturing people now not with my *kung fu* but my pen.

When I was a teenager, many young men knew some *kung fu,* or claimed to know it. The most popular style was Wing Chun, which was easy to get into but hard to excel at. Young men learned *kung fu* for self-defense and to show off, and also as a result of the domino effect. When Umbrella got beaten up by a bigger kid for being cheeky, he immediately enrolled in a Wing Chun class. Within weeks, he wanted us to accompany him to attend an arranged fight between him and some kid he had a grudge with, so that he could show off his *kung fu* moves. His opponent was a smaller kid, and Umbrella might have won that one marginally. Very soon, we heard that small kid was taking up *kung fu* as well. His *kung fu* master was the same one who taught Umbrella, so during the initiation ceremony in which that kid was to kowtow to the master and vow subservience for life, the master told Umbrella and that small kid to make up. They had their arms around each other's shoulders and swore brotherhood and allegiance to each other's life and the betterment of the art of *kung fu*. It was so disgusting to watch I almost threw up.

A younger brother of my sister's friend, also a La Salle boy, got bullied by some boys from St. George's College, which was a school for the British Army brats. He picked up Wing Chun, and apparently got to be quite good at it after a couple of years. His mission in life became going over to Kowloon Tong and picking fights with St. George's boys.

Thugs and gangsters

My favorite thug was a guy named Chee Kit who lived not too far from the wet market down Diamond Hill Road. He was a couple of years older than I was, but we were in the same class in school. He was also a Wing Chun wizard. After my dramatic improvement in academic standing in school, I let him copy my homework in exchange for protecting me from other bullies. He was everyone's friend when some extra muscles were needed. But you had to be very clear about who the target was because he had been known to mess up and beat up the wrong guy. He wasn't very bright.

Young thugs usually formed a gang and then they became formidable. There were many such loosely formed gangs. Most didn't do any harm except to protect their turf and honor, or to teach a cheeky outsider a lesson. Unlike young triad gangs nowadays, they were not into any money-making ruses, because there just wasn't any money around. They were, however, very much about girls. All the loose girls (called teddy girls) in the village were seen hanging out with them. Boys like me could only gawk and salivate.

There were basically two categories of teddy girls. One category was regular girlfriend of a thug, the other was communal property. We had a friend who was too young and too short to be a regular thug but hung around to be their errand boy. He told us he was once rewarded with one of the communal girls, but he refused in a hurry because she happened to be his older sister.

This girl had quite a past. She got knocked up at a very young age. The mother, a hawker in the wet market, when told of the pregnancy, was in for a shock because no one, not even her own daughter, could pinpoint who the father was. The young girl would offer herself for rewards as little as a ticket to a movie or a meal in a tea-house, according to Ah Ho, our maid, who knew the mother well.

The lack of privacy at home was a big problem for dating. If a boy wanted to get to know his girlfriend better, but had no car or money for a love motel, he could only use a dark corner or a deserted spot in public areas.

When I got my driver's license, the first thing my friends and I did was to borrow a car and drive it after dark to all the popular make-out spots in town, for instance, Kadoorie Avenue or dead-end streets in Ho Man Tin. We drove in without headlights and suddenly turned them on to put the spotlight on men and women in compromising positions. That was good for a cheap thrill.

The Diamond Hill thugs dealt with the privacy problem in their own way. When we were twelve or thirteen, we went gallivanting in a nearby hill and in a clearing among the bushes, the three of us stumbled upon a man and a young lady in a state of undress. Then all of a sudden, three big guys showed up and threatened to do us some harm if we didn't scram, saying we were disrupting important business their brother was conducting. We scooted away with our tails between our legs. We talked excitedly about the incident for weeks afterwards, and each time the girl was more naked than the last.

When we were a bit older, maybe fourteen or fifteen, we stumbled upon another sex scene, this time in a vacant lot where we played soccer during the day but which became deserted at night because there were no street lights. We were curious to see numerous flashlights flickering on the ground. When we went closer, we found twenty or so "couples," lying down on newspaper or towels, several feet apart, and engaging in necking and heavy petting. We didn't have a chance to have a better look, because a sentry was there pronto, and threatened to punch our eyeballs out if we looked that way again.

There were two types of thugs: the teenage bullies who ganged up to terrorize other teenagers, and the grown-up ones who were most likely triad members with prison records. I had only seen teenage thugs fighting in the streets. Adults were seen late at night in the back of a coffee shop whispering to one another. Fights usually involved several young gangsters attacking one victim. Battles between two gangs were rare, indicating that if you belonged to a gang, you didn't get bullied. The street gangs were very organized when it came to ambushing someone. A few fighters would be dispatched to guard possible escape routes. One would try to immobilize the target by bear-hugging him from behind, followed by the victim being assaulted by a barrage of fists from others. I still remember a thug by the name of Willy, who liked to strike with two fists clenched together. It must have been a pretty clumsy way to fight, but it worked well when your opponent was held down by your collaborators. The thump of fists landing on someone's body could make your heart race and give you a cold sweat.

A beating was meant to teach a lesson and not to maim. It was meant to send the victim to a bone-setter and not to a surgeon. The Chinese medicine man down the street did a swift business taking care of victims of gang attacks by applying a herbal lotion called "wine for beatings by iron" to the bruises of the battered body.

When young thugs graduated to become full-fledged adult ones, you didn't see them in the streets in broad daylight anymore. I asked one of my old acquaintances what happened to them. He said: "There is no money in Diamond Hill." They often migrated to Mong Kok, Yau Ma Tei, and Tsim Sha Tsui where all the money-making actions were.

Umbrella's neighbor was a Chiu Chow triad member of good standing. He was typical in that he married a plain-looking school teacher, a homebody who bore him children and looked after him without questioning him about his whereabouts or his businesses. He ran an illegal gambling den, and sometimes took Umbrella and me on a tour of all the joints where he had "influence," including a dance hall in Yau Ma Tei where he talked to the manager in a dialect I couldn't understand even though it was Cantonese. He collected $10 each from us, and he only used half of the money when it was time to pay and pocketed the rest. Umbrella told me the big man was accustomed to getting discounts wherever he went.

The relationship between policemen and thugs was complicated, especially with Chiu Chow men. It was said the career path of a Chiu Chow boy would be either a gangster or a cop—the former a regular thug, the latter a thug with a gun and a warrant card. A Chiu

Chow boy of age could apply to the police academy if he hadn't had a criminal record and was semi-literate. Failing that, he would join some relatives or childhood friends in what would be called *lo pin moon,* which could be loosely translated into "working in a semi-legal business."

I had seen gangsters arrested by policemen and the verbal exchange would be in the Chiu Chow dialect, with the gangsters declaring their affiliations, looking for some kind of connection. Violence broke out often, usually with the gangster punching the cop. I seldom witnessed police brutality in the streets, but I was told if you were in the much feared *tsap tsai fong*—the room of the plain-clothed Criminal Investigation Division officers, you would be in for an experience you wouldn't forget.

The beat policemen in our eyes were pretty low human beings. They were, as I alluded to before, thugs with a license. I had seen them walk into Tai Lin's place, an open house, pick up an apple off the dinner table and walk away. They did their route, stopped by a few illegal spots to collect their daily bribes and did nothing except bully female hawkers. Umbrella's father knew a few cops, and that was how we learnt of the illegal gambling and opium dens in the neighborhood.

The plain-clothed CID were even worse; their demeanor was indistinguishable from that of triad thugs, with their true identity apparent only when they showed off the gun they carried at the waist.

Many thugs wore hats, the kind you see in Humphrey Bogart movies. We watched a policeman trying to chase down a thug, and dramatically the hat fell off his head, and that stopped the policeman in his tracks, because he had to pick up the hat and look for clues inside. Some older guy told us, in a conspiratorial tone, that there would be a hundred-dollar bill tucked inside.

Not all young thugs grew up to be professional gangsters. A guy by the name of Johnson used to go out with my sister. (As was usually the case, a La Salle boy and a Maryknoll girl). He lived in Kowloon City but came to Diamond Hill often because of my sister. He was a muscular guy and was much feared among the young thugs in Diamond Hill, because he teamed up with another La Salle boy by the name of Michael who lived in Tai Hom Village, and together they had broken a few bones and taught a few lessons to the local teddy boys. Johnson later in life migrated to Canada and became an accountant. And Michael became Mr. Michael Hui Koon Man, the showbiz tycoon, and one of the most successful comic actors and movie producers Hong Kong has seen. Michael has three younger brothers. The oldest one was Hui Koon Mo, nicknamed "Hero," who in those days formed his own youth gang terrorizing the neighborhood. He grew up more law-abiding but did no better than being the owner of unsuccessful bars and restaurants. The other two younger brothers were not like Hero; they were more like Michael and went into show biz. Hui Koon Ying became a comic actor, and the youngest brother is Samuel Hui Koon Kit, the most famous of the brothers, who had an illustrious music career, and is still lauded by Hong Kong people as the god of Canto pop.

A dog's life

I GREW UP IN DIAMOND HILL having to deal with dogs, and I have kept on having to deal with them for most of my life.

There are dogs in my life now, because my wife is an animal lover. She started out with cats, but is now more into dogs. I'm glad, because I think dogs are more deserving of love and devotion. With dogs, every time you get home, there is a welcoming party. Cats are usually asleep when you enter through the door. And if they are awake, they make you feel you have neglected them all day or you have wakened them up for nothing.

My wife first adopted an abandoned cat, and within months convinced me that having two cats in the house was better because they could play with each other and therefore would leave the furniture alone. We ended up with two cats playing with the furniture. She named them Ling Ling and Onyx. They follow their favorite person like a bad smell but deny my existence. I call them Ding-a-ling and Onerous.

Then a stray dog she named Brownie followed her home, and she took him in "just for a few days" so that she could find him a home. She sure did—our home. Then she found a stray puppy in a gutter after a rainstorm and adopted her, too. I knew what was coming when she gave the newcomer a name—Mappie. I finally put my foot down and threatened to move out if any more pets were to come.

Every evening after dinner, my wife would be surrounded by love: two cats on her lap and two dogs at her feet. Sometimes she throws a little crumpet my way and cuddles with me; members of her fan club give me dirty looks.

My stepmother was also an animal lover. Her pets were a lot like surrogate children since she had no children of her own. We always had a cat and a dog at home. She adopted our first dog, Mabel, who was a cross between a Basset Hound and something else.

My father was the sedentary type of guy and my stepmom was always tired. Ah Ho, our maid, was born to play mahjong. My sisters didn't go outside unless clearly necessary. I was low in the totem pole, and naturally walking the dog became my calling.

A dog's life

Mabel was with us for five or six years, and I walked her every evening during the whole period. That came to about two thousand times.

We took the same route each time. We went up Diamond Hill Road, crossed the bridge to Sheung Yuen Ling, where there was a row of fancy apartments inhabited by Portuguese and British families. Past that was the one-lane road exiting at Ngau Chi Wan and leading to the rest of Kowloon. I usually turned back at the top of that road and headed back home, unless I decided to stay away from home longer, then we would go further up the road and enter the hilly areas by crossing another bridge.

I always used a leash on Mabel because there were just too many dogs in the area, including the strays in our neighborhood and the domesticated ones in the fancy apartments at Sheung Yuen Ling. My prudence was vindicated when one time my stepmom walked Mabel, and she didn't use the leash. She came back home in tears, and I overheard her telling my father that Mabel "was taken." The conventional Chinese thinking at that time was that anytime a female had sex with a male, even though consensual, she was taken advantage of. Apparently, Mabel in heat and without a leash was taken by a male dog. The perpetrator was from the Sheung Yuen Ling district. It happened so fast my stepmom did not have time to pour cold water on them to separate them.

A few months later, we had a handful of puppies in our hands. Fortunately, they were all adopted easily. The puppies looked like the Dalmatian belonging to Michael Costa who lived in Sheung Yuen Ling. Michael was a Portuguese boy also studying in La Salle. He had movie-star good looks and was very popular with the girls. He married young to a British girl even younger, who studied at King George V, the school of choice for expatriate children. He had to marry her because she got pregnant, and her father was a lawyer. It appeared that Sheung Yuen Ling was a fertile neighborhood indeed.

There were strays that hung around, that were given names and scraps of leftover food. Then there were itinerant strays that were fair game, meaning they could be anyone's free meal. In a way, that was how the population of stray dogs was controlled.

Neutering of dogs was unheard of. We imposed contraception on them by enforcing celibacy. Everyone had a mandate to beat the dogs to break them up when a male tried to mount a bitch. And if it had already gone beyond that stage, plan B was to dump cold water on them. It was not unusual to find in street corners two wet dogs with their rear ends stuck together, standing there facing opposite directions, and wondering what the heck had happened.

With my sick sense of humor even at that age, I had thought about dishing out the same treatment to my fellow human beings, just to look at their faces.

We did spay cats, though. Not so much for controlling the cat population, but for the more selfish reason of wanting to have quiet nights. Female cats in heat and in sexual intercourse made a noise like bloody murder no one could sleep through. Once in a while, service was required of an itinerant "cat doctor" who came by the neighborhood, selling his service by loudly broadcasting his trade in euphemistic terms.

The operation was swift and inexpensive. The cat was first strapped and tied down in something like a strait-jacket, exposing her belly. The "doctor" scraped off some hair from the belly, exposing the skin and then made a small cut on it with a scalpel. With expert ease, he next picked up the ovaries with forceps and cut them off with scissors. No anesthesia, no sutures, no drugs, no sweat. Having seen how the old-timers operated, I wonder if vets today are making a big deal out of that simple procedure and are overcharging us.

Like neutering, picking up after your own dog was also an unknown concept, but Mabel was good enough not to ever get me into trouble by always doing her business in places nobody minded. We had a system. If I refused to move, Mabel knew that spot was as good as any to use as her toilet. She was a good dog. We ignored each other at home, but we were buddies once we were out.

Mabel and I had a symbiotic relationship. She needed to get out once in a while; I needed her as an excuse to get out once in a while. The walks were in many ways therapeutic for me. But all good things must come to an end. Mabel got on in age, and started to become frail. Soon after she developed a skin disease, which was probably a manifestation of something more sinister inside her body. She died in her sleep, by my stepmom's bed.

I gave her a last walk, in a trolley.

I was never afraid of dead bodies. While all other household members felt squeamish about touching dead Mabel, I shoved her inside an old hemp sack previously used to hold rice, with the help of Ah Fai, grandson of Ah Ho. We then pushed the trolley along Mabel's favorite route, crossing that bridge, passing the fancy apartments and turning up to the trail leading to the hills. We went far enough so that there were no more village houses in sight. We had brought along a shovel, and with it we dug a deep hole, lowered

Mabel into it, and then covered her with soil. It was drizzling when we started the journey, and it was pouring by the time the burial was finished. I told Ah Fai, who was a few years younger than I was that it was the sky mourning for Mabel. The heavy rain came in handy; nobody could notice the tears running down my cheeks.

Not long after, my stepmom adopted another dog, a Chow Chow we named Michael. I didn't walk him as often as with Mabel, because by then I was a big boy and didn't need any excuse to get out.

This dog was a biter. My stepmother, who preferred feeding her pets by hand, got bitten feeding him. When confronted with a stick, he bit the stick. What a feisty little dog. He bit everyone in the household, and when he bit the hands that fed him one time too many, it was the last straw and he was given the boot. He was given to a factory owner who needed a guard dog at his factory on the other side of Diamond Hill, miles away.

I left home to live in the university hostel at nineteen, and was not there during the later part of Michael's life. According to my sister, Michael found his way home after a few months. My stepmom opened the door one day and found Michael waiting to get in. The first thing he did once inside the house was to jump on his favorite chair in the house and lie there sleeping.

He looked different, not only older, but transformed as if someone had performed plastic surgery on him. My family took him back. We couldn't get rid of him after that. As he got older, he became mellow and didn't bite anymore. He died a couple of years later, preceded by a skin ailment just like Mabel. He was taken to the RSPCA when he was terminal, where he was put down. I wasn't home to give him the same ceremonial burial though.

Not many dogs in Diamond Hill were as lucky as Mabel and Michael. There were many semi-feral dogs that lived on leftovers, which were hard to come by in my neighborhood. In times of hardship, a dog's life is just that.

All the feral dogs were Chinese breeds. They were known to be intelligent, loyal and unfortunately, edible. Foreign dogs such as Dalmatian or Alsatian, Chihuahua or Chow Chow, Pomeranian or Pekinese, even mixed breeds of them, usually could find a home. No one would eat foreign dogs either, because their meat was considered "poisonous." They were the lucky ones.

Tai Lin's neighbors, a mean couple who bullied Tai Lin's family for years, had a Chinese dog called Ah

Choi, a common name for both dogs and male servants in that era. (The use of the auspicious name, which means fortune, hopes to bring in some of that.)

One day, the couple decided they were too hungry to wait for fortune to knock on their door; so instead, they knocked Fortune with a hammer, so that they could at least have food on the table. The wife, a petite woman, did such a clumsy job in executing the kill that a small crowd gathered around their front porch. The husband, feeling perhaps threatened or embarrassed, or a bit of both, went around asking everyone: "Is there a problem?" That dog, in the final moments of his life, must have wondered what he did wrong to deserve that.

Having dog meat on the menu might be illegal, but the authorities seemed to turn a blind eye to the practice. Some *dai pai dong*s, like those in Temple Street, would hang a goat's head up front—a signal for customers to know that dog meat was on the menu.

In a lawless place like the Walled City, dog meat was openly available. They even had a code name for it—*sam-luk* (three and six in Cantonese, which add up to nine, *gow*, sounding exactly like "dog").

Not everyone was as cruel as Tai Lin's neighbors, the couple who ate their own pet dog. But when a stray dog walked past a few hungry young men, anything could happen. It was usually a group activity in the open, with camaraderie and division of labor. One person would start the fire and boil water in a big pot. The expert would be asked to do the gutting, skinning and cleaning. Someone would volunteer to buy the vegetables, sauces and spices. Any passersby would be invited to join in, to share the food and the blame if something went wrong.

Hey! Wait a minute. Why are you looking at me like that? I never said I was there.

Hollywood in Diamond Hill

I N THE 1960S, HONG KONG WAS the capital of the world in making movies. In 1963, for example, the government was quick to boast in its annual report that this backwater city on the China coast produced 310 feature films, while America produced only 155.

Diamond Hill was home to movie studios that made hundreds of Cantonese and Mandarin movies and had genuinely earned the title: "Hollywood of the East." The biggest studio and the one I visited most often was Tai Koon (Grandview) Studio. Another one was called Wah Tat Studio, owned by Tso Tat-wah, the actor cursed by the gambling bug, who lost it all in poker and blackjack.

Even though everyone in Diamond Hill knew there were movie studios in the neighborhood, not too many people were excited about their presence or the proximity of movie stars. I was not aware of any grown-up bothering to spend an afternoon there star-gazing. They all had better things to do, such as making a living or playing mahjong.

I went there sometimes only when I had absolutely nothing else to do.

When my friend took me to Tai Koon Studio for the first time, I was surprised that the entrance was a dilapidated arch with the name of the studio painted on the two narrow pillars and the paint had seen better days. There were no guards at the entrance; one could just walk in. It was not a glamorous place by any standard. There were trees and gardens and low-rise office buildings around but the inside of the studio itself looked like a barn—spacious, rustic, with a tall ceiling and a dirt floor. There were electric wires all over the place and it seemed the most important thing was lighting. A lot of people spent a lot of time in arranging the lights.

We waited and waited, but nothing seemed to be happening. A lot of people were milling around and the scene could be best described as chaotic. The stars on that day were second- or third-tier Mandarin actors and actresses and they were in a modern drama involving a young lady who worked as a lowly clerk for a company boss who was trying to win her heart.

But the son of the company boss was the one she was truly in love with. I knew the plot well because I had seen Chinese movies with more or less the same plot many times before. I also knew who the stars were even though not by name because they were the ones wearing heavy make-up. They were sitting in a corner, and were constantly fussed over by the make-up artists who were either touching up their faces with additional cosmetics or messing with their hair.

The tea lady brought in some fruit apparently paid for by some visiting actor who was a friend of one of the female stars. All the workers dropped whatever they were doing and zoomed in on the fruit.

All that waiting was killing me, and I was not having fun.

After a long while, someone (the director, I presumed) yelled "Camera!" and everyone perked up and kept quiet. The scene involved the son confronting the father about his paramour, with his mother on his side. All three actors were standing and facing the camera in a rather awkward way, but that was movie making in that era for you. The scene ended with the mother leading the father away by pulling on his ear and cursing him. The next scene showed the son taking over the company, and reuniting with the love of his life. There was a lot of acting (and overacting) for one afternoon.

I asked my friend, who was older and a frequent visitor to the studio, why the cameraman seemed to be so well respected. He told me that was because he could make an actor or actress look better or worse by determining the angle of the shoot, and that actresses often had to offer themselves to him for that favor. That might not have been true, but that kind of talk certainly appealed to my teenage mind.

Outtakes were uncommon, and if they happened, I was told, they could be for generating more footage of that scene for the benefit of another movie in production with a similar plot by the same actors in the next studio.

I had been to other studios and they were all alike. They seemed to let anyone in. There was no security to speak of. If you were fifteen years old, you obviously didn't belong, and someone might tap you on the shoulder and ask you why you were there. I got around that little problem by claiming to be a relative of Jin Yong, aka Louis Cha, the famous *kung fu* writer who started a business making movies out of his popular novels. That was around the same time I was also name-dropping to get free bus rides.

The cinema business was booming in the 50s and 60s in Hong Kong. There was nothing much else in terms of entertainment for the masses. Boys and girls dating found the dark cinema the perfect venue to have some kind of privacy.

There were broadly three types of movies shown in cinemas: Cantonese, Mandarin, and English.

The Cantonese ones were considered low-brow and vulgar, and favored by the Cantonese but no one else. Depending on what actors and actresses wore, the Cantonese films could be classified as modern or ancient. The ancient ones could be Cantonese operas, or well-known historical stories mixed with some *kung fu* scenes. The modern ones were love stories mixed with comedies, or mysteries and whodunit detective stories. All had predictable story lines and endings. The modern *kung fu* genre came later on, first in Mandarin classics such as *Dragon Gate Inn,* and the *The One-Armed Swordsman,* followed by Bruce Lee's successful series until his untimely death in the 70s. Louis Cha's novel-based movies were more for TV because they were epics. Jackie Chan came much later. He was, by his own admission, Charlie Chaplin with *kung fu* moves.

Cantonese movies for the longest time were in black and white, with horrible sound tracks. The actors were all set in their roles. Clowns would always be clowns, and villains would always be villains. One actor by the name of Shek Kin played the villain so well and for so long that when he appeared in public, he would be jeered and sometimes assaulted by the crowd. The iconic couple, Yam Kim-fai and Pak Suet-sin, both ladies, appeared in so many pictures together playing lovers with Yam playing the male role, that in real life, they were regarded as such. Neither one of them married. When Yam died in 1989, she bequeathed all her worldly possessions, worth many millions of dollars, to Pak who for her part acted the grieving widow by weeping uncontrollably during the funeral and for days after.

The Mandarin movies in the 50s and 60s were more sophisticated productions. They were the first local movies in color. They were usually love stories with theme songs which became hits with the Mandarin speaking fans. Those movies frequently dominated awards ceremonies held in Taiwan. One famous award-winning movie was *Endless Love* with Lin Dai playing the lead actress role and also singing the theme song of the same name. The song remained the number-one hit for months.

There were two main movie production companies competing against each other. One was Cathay, owned by the Malaysian tycoon Loke Wan Tho, and the other was the Shaw Brothers owned by Run Run Shaw and his brothers. The two companies were the driving force behind the Mandarin movie business. Run Run Shaw's older brother, Shao Zuiweng, was the visionary. He was making movies in Shanghai before the Japanese war when Shanghai was the center of the universe. He foresaw the potential of Cantonese movies because Cantonese was the common dialect of all the overseas Chinese, especially in southeast Asia. He sent his younger brother Run Run to Singapore to set up a movie studio to make Cantonese movies, but the endeavor was foiled by the Japanese war. After the war, Run Run came to Hong Kong in the 1950s. By then the movie business in Shanghai was non-existent, and he immediately built a studio in Clearwater Bay, and took center stage in the movie business world in Hong Kong. He made both Mandarin and Cantonese movies. He lured the best talents and contracted the most beautiful Mandarin-speaking actresses, including Lin Dai, Lin Chuey, Yul Min, and Lin Po. His movies were also big box office successes.

One thing about these female Mandarin stars was that suicide attempts by them seemed to be frequent. Every so often, I read in the newspaper about these, usually by drug overdose. Some tried several times.

One was quoted in the newspaper saying that she would never do it again, not because of a spiritual enlightenment, but because while she was semi-comatose in the ambulance, the three ambulance men took turns molesting her. Lin Dai was the only one I know who succeeded after several attempts, and died in the late 60s. Nowadays, her name elicits more emotion and nostalgia for her suicide than her movies. Her family never moved her belongings from her luxurious flat on Hong Kong Island, until recently, when they were moved to a government-sponsored venue for public display, in the name of cultural preservation.

Movies in English had the biggest slice of the box office revenue. *Ben Hur, The Sound of Music, Cleopatra, My Fair Lady, From Russia with Love, West Side Story,* and other big Hollywood productions, all made a killing. The English movies were favored by the younger generation because of the elitist mentality. Students from elite schools wouldn't want to be caught dead in a cinema showing a Cantonese, or for that matter, a Mandarin movie.

Over the years, innumerable Western films had used the streets of Hong Kong as a backdrop. A few of them were actually made in Hong Kong. Clark Gable and Susan Hayward came and made *Soldier of*

Fortune. William Holden and Jennifer Jones came and made *Love is a Many-Splendored Thing*. And the most famous of all—*The World of Suzie Wong*—in which the lead actress was Hong Kong-born Nancy Kwan, a beautiful Eurasian. Newspapers never tired of reporting visits by major Hollywood stars. They often told and retold the story of Clark Gable in the Peninsula Hotel bar ordering a "screwdriver" and getting the kind from a handyman's tool box. When Hollywood stars came to town, they were given the kind of media coverage local stars could only dream of. They were usually entertained by the local movie studio bosses, who used them to bring publicity to their local stars by having group photos. But there was never any doubt who the real stars were: West was best.

For the same reason, secondary school students, especially those in English medium schools, followed popular singers from Western countries, especially the US. First there were Patti Page and Doris Day, singing cute songs such as *Changing Partners* and *Tennessee Waltz, How Much is that Doggie in the Window,* and *Que Sera, Sera*. Pat Boone and Elvis Presley were popular for a long time. Pat Boone was popular because of his clean-cut image and one could sing his songs easily. Elvis was even more popular because of his bad-boy image and iconoclastic status. His hair-style—the sides swept towards the back in a duck tail and a few strands of hair hung down the forehead, all held in place by industrial strength hair grease, was widely imitated, and bad boys (called teddy boys) also tried to dress like him, in jeans, white leather shoes, and (gasp!) bright red socks. When Elvis was drafted into the military, he had to follow the rules and cut his hair short. He received special permission to don a unique hair-style—long on the sides, and short on top. All of a sudden, we saw the same flat-top hairdo all over the city. He topped the local pop chart on a regular basis with songs such as *Jailhouse Rock, Blue Suede Shoes,* and *Love Me Tender.* He lost his popu-larity after he grew fat and started to sing those Hawaiian songs. It didn't help that the whole world, including Hong Kong, was invaded in later years by British groups such as The Beatles, The Rolling Stones, The Dave Clark Five and The Animals. Non-vocal instrumental groups such as The Ventures and The Shadows were also popular. Unlucky for them, with the Chinese finding the "v" and "sh" difficult to pronounce, they became The Wentures and The Sad-dles. By the time The Beatles visited Hong Kong, I was in my late teens and old enough to go to pubs, and wherever I went, the jukebox would be blasting their music or that of one of the other British groups. *The House of the Rising Sun* by The Animals was particularly popular, and was played over and over again.

The older Westernized generation also liked English songs, by singers such as Bing Crosby, Frank Sinatra, Nat King Cole, or the opera singer Mario Lanza. They disapproved of Elvis because of what he did with his hips. They disapproved of The Beatles because of their funny hairstyle and their irreverence, and for that matter all modern singers because "they didn't make singers like they used to."

Local youths formed musical groups, invariably playing rock and roll modeled after Western bands with lead guitar, rhythm, bass and drums. Though not too many aspiring musicians were talented, many formed bands to impress their friends and to meet girls. Having the opportunity to perform in a band and provide music at a party for high school kids almost guaranteed leaving the party with the phone numbers of a few adoring teenage girls. Even Tai Lin, someone with serious self-esteem problems, became very popular with the girls after he joined a band as a singer. He was quite good, and he specialized in lovey-dovey songs. He told me he would reserve *Let It Be Me* by José Feliciano to propose to the love of his life. It must have worked because he later married one of his fans, and remains happily married to her today.

I also tried like hell to get into a band. My problem was that I didn't have the dexterity and the rhythm to play the guitar well and I couldn't carry a tune to save my life. For once I agreed with my father—I had better stick with getting a good education.

Organizing dance parties was basically the domain of students from elite English medium schools. And since the popular dances were rock-n-roll, cha-cha, and the twist, Western music was a pre-requisite. Students with poor knowledge of English would not have a clue about such music.

Anything in English was more prestigious. The standard of English in those days, in my opinion, was not as high as today in spite of all the complaints we hear from many quarters to the contrary. There were far fewer English speakers then, but those who were proficient might have been better than today's average English speakers. You didn't see or hear horrendously bad English as often as today because those who didn't know English well would not write it publicly and would keep their mouths shut.

When I was thirteen or fourteen, I was on a bus heading home. A Western couple, the kind-looking missionary type, asked the fare collector for directions, but he couldn't understand anything they said, so he went around asking all the passengers for help, until I volunteered and told them they could get off at the end of the line. Today, no doubt more people on any bus would be able to help.

There are also a lot more people speaking perfect English today, because more parents can afford to send their children to international schools in Hong Kong or schools in Western countries to study at a young age when their language learning ability peaks. Far fewer youngsters had the opportunity to go abroad in my day.

In general, apart from students in English medium schools, and the well-educated Shanghainese clan, most Hong Kong people in the 50s and 60s were Cantonese speakers with poor knowledge of either English or Mandarin.

That was why Cantonese movies had a wide fan base in spite of the poor quality of the film-making. Each movie was scheduled to show in the cinemas for only one week or less before being replaced by another one. Movie studios cranked out movies fast, at the rate of, I kid you not, as many as two a week.

I was not a fan of Cantonese movies. They were all so predictable and embarrassingly dorky. Tso Tat-wah, for example, when playing the police detective, always solved the crime he was working on in the last minute, by finger-pointing the villain, without giving the reason or the logic behind his coup, saying only that he had always been suspicious of that person. The villain always resisted arrest and would take a swing at Tso, which he clumsily but always successfully ducked. Tso would then return the favor which would always connect and the villain then had no choice but to surrender.

It was all so unconvincing. I met Tso Tat-wah in the flesh around the blackjack table on numerous occasions. He was so puny I could take his lunch money.

When he played a *kung fu* master, the special effects were so awful the movie might as well have been a comedy.

I was more interested in the young Cantonese actresses, such as Fung Bo-bo, Siu Fong-fong, Chan Po-chu, and Sit Ka-yin. They were all about my age, and they were hot. But they were seldom seen in the movie studios. Instead, I often ran into old Cantonese actors like the avuncular Leung Sing-bo, or that witch of a woman, Wong Man-lei, who always played the heinous mother-in-law.

Actors, especially for Cantonese movies were very down-to-earth. When I developed the studying habit of sleeping during the day and burning the midnight oil until the wee hours, my reward for the hard work was to saunter down Diamond Hill road to the wet market area and to have a bowl of congee in one of the all-night *dai pai dong*s. And there I would encounter some of the big names in cinema eating at the next table after a hard day of filming, some still with heavy make-up on.

When a Cantonese movie required an outdoor scene, for example, a mob traveling from the town hall to someone's residence to find fault with him, a procession of people led by actors playing village leaders would jostle along a narrow path by the hillside. Soon the procession would grow longer and longer when spectators from all over joined in and followed the leaders. In other words, we were working as extras for free without realizing it. Then came some clueless person who wanted to join in but ran down the path towards the mob from the opposite direction and ruined the shot. The "village leaders" chided that errant unwelcome "extra" for wasting so much film they could have used the money to treat all the villagers to a free meal if it wasn't for his foul-up.

In case you wonder why I know so much about the situation, I have a confession to make. I was the genius behind the above-mentioned foul-up.

Everything seemed amateurish, but Hollywood Diamond-Hill-style was charming nonetheless, and many films became classics. Cantonese movies have become more and more sophisticated over the years, and Hollywood is now coming to Hong Kong to look for new ideas and new techniques. A few Hong Kong movie stars in recent years have become international stars. They wouldn't have such achievements without their predecessors paving the way in Diamond Hill.

The Walled City and the
white powder

AH FUI IS A NATIVE HAKKA, a very passive and meek Chinese ethnic group. Hakka means foreigners in their own land, that's why they invented the walled villages to ward off outside invaders. I always remember that because when we first met, Ah Fui told me he lived near the Walled City, and I thought he meant one of those Hakka ones.

When I was attending La Salle, Kowloon City was within walking distance; so sometimes I stopped by his home after school, looking for trouble. We made trips into one of the most literally lawless places in the world—the Walled City.

Kowloon Walled City had a rich history. It was built in the nineteenth century originally as an administrative office of the Qing dynasty to govern the region stretching from Shenzhen to Lantau Island.

The wall was built after the British government took over Hong Kong, but was taken down when Japan took over Hong Kong during the war. The Japanese military needed the stones from the wall to build the foundation for an extension of the Kai Tak Airport.

In 1898, when the British leased the New Territories from the Chinese government for ninety-nine years, the Walled City was not part of the deal. The status of the Walled City had always been ambiguous. In my day it was commonly known as the zone of three non-interventions, that is, no intervention from the judiciary, law enforcement agencies and the Inland Revenue Department. In theory, it was not under the jurisdiction of the British government; and it was sort of off limits to the policemen. Home owners there did not have to pay government rates.

Mainland trained dentists could practice there without a license, hence it was also known as the place to go for inexpensive dental care.

One of the largest triad societies in Hong Kong today originated from there. The head of that group was from Chiu Chow, and supposedly started the organization as a patriotic anti-communism force. The organization he started gradually evolved to become a triad society with members spilling out of the Walled City into other areas of Hong Kong. He had a number of sons who all became high-profile triad figures decades after the father's death.

Chiu Chow gangs ruled the place, and the Chiu Chow influence was reflected in the large number of their restaurants at the periphery of the Walled City. After its demolition, some of the Chiu Chow restaurants moved across the street to Kowloon City.

Ah Fui had a relative who used to live in the Walled City. He was only a few years older than we were but acted a lot older. I had to call him Mr. Chow to show respect. He had flair in telling stories, and liked to close his eyes, shake his head slowly and make *tsk tsk* noises when he thought the story had reached its climax.

He used to work for a triad boss who organized striptease shows performed on an open-air bamboo scaffolding stage within the Walled City. His job was to market the show to pedestrians along the sidewalks at the periphery of the city, by telling men of all ages in a hushed tone that a wonderful show had been scheduled at a certain hour that night. Sometimes he had to go as far as Yau Ma Tei near Temple Street to bring in customers. The show had the usual components of a striptease: four or five girls coming on stage one by one, the music, the progressive disrobing, and the finale when the performer turned around facing the audience in her birthday suit. He took half an hour to describe each act, adding details about the performers' physical attributes and their studied coyness. He even hummed the music for us, and simulated the moves.

The entry fee for the show was five dollars, quite a lot of money for the 50s. But the shows were there not for the relatively small profit made for the underworld bosses, but for enticing people with money to spare to other activities sponsored by them—gambling and drugs. Mr. Chow knew everything about these two trades, because he had run errands for the bosses when he was a kid. And he took pleasure in imparting his knowledge to younger boys like Ah Fui and me.

The most popular games played there were Russian poker and *fan-tan*. In Russian poker, every player is dealt thirteen cards, and by arranging the cards in three-five-five order, whoever is the stronger in two or more of the combination wins the hand. *Fan-tan* starts with a pile of beads. One can bet from one to four or any combination of the four numbers. By taking away four beads at a time, the remaining number of beads four or under becomes the winning number. It is a simple but exciting game because of the gradual building up of tension during the counting process.

Drugs in the Walled City were of three kinds: opium, *hung yuan* (the red pill), and heroin (in Cantonese parlance *paak fan,* white powder). Though all three were opiate derivatives, the *paak fan* was by far the most popular. Hong Kong addicts didn't inject heroin then, they inhaled it, and there were three ways to do it. The first way was called "chasing the dragon." It started with heating up the heroin and a powder base on tin foil (easily found in cigarette packages), and when the mixture turned liquid and then vapor, the addict chased after the vapor frantically with a straw and sucked it all in.

The second method was called "playing the harmonica." The heating up process was the same as the first method, but it started out with a larger quantity of white powder, and the tool used for inhaling was the outer box of the old-fashioned matchbox. The big square opening allowed the addict to inhale quickly a large quantity of vapor and as a result get a quicker and bigger hit. The "harmonica players" were big spenders and operators of the *paak fan* stands often pushed aside the "dragon chasers" to make room for them. Such stands were known as "recharge stations," because addicts used them to restore their energy.

The third way to take heroin was used by addicts when outside the Walled City, where a blatant act of cooking and inhaling the drug could be asking for trouble from the police. This method involved using an ordinary cigarette with the tobacco partially replaced by *paak fan* . In burning and inhaling it, one had to keep the cigarette pointing towards the sky to avoid spillage, so this method was called "firing the missile."

Mr. Chow had seen it all. He promised to take Ah Fui and me to visit his old haunt and Ah Fui told him we were interested only in the striptease and not the other stuff. He said they didn't do that anymore, because there were so many places in the sex trade outside the Walled City no one cared about the strip show. There were the occasional live shows and blue movies though, and he would let us know.

He was a man of his word. One afternoon while Ah Fui and I were playing cards he called for us to meet him downstairs.

It was still early, and he had to run a few errands, so we tagged along to have a tour of the place.

There was one entrance to the Walled City not too far from Hau Wong Road where Ah Fui lived. The entrance was narrow and almost hidden. The whole city was full of tortuous lanes. Occasional bicycles were seen, but there was no thoroughfare wide enough for a car.

The Walled City and the white powder

The entire Walled City was not a sin city. The western part was inhabited by people who woke up early in the morning and went to bed before midnight. They held regular jobs outside the city or owned businesses or factories inside the city producing simple hand-made merchandise. People from this part never ventured into the middle and eastern part, and they were pretty much left alone. Mr. Chow had to go drop something off to his parents who lived in the western side. There were young children playing in the front yard and housewives collecting items from the clotheslines. The place was no different from Diamond Hill.

The eastern part of the city was a different story. It was darker and gloomier. The paths seemed more dilapidated and wet. Gutters were everywhere, heavily infested with rats, some dead, some alive. The place was deserted, but Mr. Chow assured us it would come alive after dark. As we walked through he pointed to a street on our left called Kwong Ming Street which could be translated into "Bright" Street. This street was dark and gloomy in broad daylight, but became bright after dark because there would be scores of lit candles on top of all the "recharge stations" set up along the narrow road for addicts to cook heroin.

Mr. Chow pointed to another lane where *sam-luk* was sold at night. Ah Fui asked where the brothels were, and Mr. Chow, being his older cousin, gave him a disapproving look and moved on without giving us an answer.

Soon we reached our destination.

The porn house could have been a living room on the ground floor of a village house. There were rows of home-made benches facing a stage. Mr. Chow chit-chatted to the people there in Chiu Chow dialect briefly and left us there. We took our seats, joining the ten or so other young men already there.

There were two shows that day: a blue movie followed by a live show. The young man who ran the show was in his late teens and he was a comedian. He collected money from us and cracked jokes while doing it. Even without Mr. Chow as our protector, we didn't feel threatened at any time.

The black and white movie featured a cripple chasing a scantily clothed girl through the jungle. The girl kept on tripping and falling, and the cripple almost caught her a hundred times. Towards the end of the movie, we didn't care anymore. We wished some big jungle beast would eat them up, to end our misery.

The live show was livelier. One woman demon-
strated her ability to smoke cigarettes simultaneously
from both ends of her body. Another played a musical
instrument. One performed sex acts that involved a
snake, and another one could shoot a dart to pop a
balloon. At the end of the show, there was bleeding, from
both the performers and their props. The performers
were unattractive and obviously heroin junkies. All in
all, the performances were freakish and not erotic at
all. They did nothing for me, except giving me brag-
ging rights to tell other teenage boys that I had seen
it all.

Ah Fui and I went back there a few more times on
our own, but soon got tired of the same nonsense. But
we never dared to go there after dark.

Adults warned us repeatedly about the Walled City,
not so much about the pornography and prostitution
there, but the *paak fan* trade. They told us horror
stories about young boys and girls lured or forced into
addiction to become captive couriers for the heroin
kingpin. I never stayed in the Walled City long
enough to witness any incident related to the heroin
trade, but there was enough of that in Diamond Hill.

Twin brothers I knew had a hard life growing up
with their widower father, who liked to beat them

with a rattan rod for no reason, and then beat them some more for crying because of the beating.

One time the three of us went to explore a village a few miles from Diamond Hill on a Sunday afternoon. We came to a fork in the road. One twin went one way with me, the other, just to be different, went the other. We met up again later in the day. The wayward twin was very excited about what he had discovered. He had stumbled upon an opium den, and he made an easy five bucks, a lot of money for a kid, for running errands.

You guess the rest. At eighteen, he had already become a hardened heroin addict. He died not too long ago, after having been in and out of jail many times. His brother managed to stay out of trouble and is now a successful accountant. He and I were lucky not to have picked that road and faced temptation on that fateful day.

I worked briefly in a drug rehab center in the US, and a methadone clinic part-time in Hong Kong. Over the years I have learned a thing or two about heroin addiction. It is one powerful addiction, especially if taken intravenously. When the drug hits the vein, you get a high comparable to an orgasm in pleasure, intensity and duration. After a calming-down phase, you go through a nodding phase. With eyes closed, and body totally relaxed, you sway back and forth and nod your head. You can be so relaxed sometimes you wet yourself. Some addicts at this stage start thinking about making money for the next hit.

So next time you see a thin unkempt man bobbing his head and squatting in a pool of urine with a begging bowl in front of him, you know what that is about.

Few things can be as self-destructive as heroin addiction. Men become thieves; women become prostitutes. The change of personality after heroin addiction is tell-tale. The only thing I can say about them is that although they seem nice enough and deserve sympathy, they can never be trusted.

A guy nicknamed Tai Kou in the neighborhood was a big kid and was known never to back down from a fight. No one messed with him. Though about my age, he was more inclined to interact with adults, and wouldn't have the time of day for a kid like me. All that changed one day when he waited at the entrance to Diamond Hill and accosted me. I took one look at him and knew he had become a *paak fan* addict. He put an arm around my shoulder as if we were long-lost best friends and engaged me in small talk. I knew what was coming but couldn't get away without "lending" him my pocket change. That was typical of a heroin addict, using a mixture of threats and charm to get money for the next hit.

There were far more male addicts than female ones, but when a young girl got hooked, it evoked more drama and gossip. A young vegetable vendor in the wet market got arrested by police one day, and rumors had it she was a hardened heroin addict and was making more money on the side selling drugs than vegetables. She went to jail for a while, and was not seen in the wet market again. Her last sighting was in the streets of Mong Kok, selling herself.

The younger brother of someone I played mahjong with got hooked at a very young age. The father was devastated, and turned to everyone he could think of for help. I was in university by then. He traveled all the way to Pok Fu Lam to the hostel where I boarded to beg me to help his boy. He was in tears and on the verge of kneeling in front of me if I could offer help in any way. I was a lowly undergrad with no means or influence, and could not offer him any magic bullet solution to rid his son of his demon. But I did urge him to consider sending his son back to Mainland China. Once in there, addicts would have no choice but to quit cold turkey. Then they made them work so hard in the re-education camp that they would not have any time to think about such nonsense as putting heroin into their veins.

I lost contact with them since that last visit. I do not know what happened to the boy, but I sure felt for the father who was paying dearly for the sins of his son.

Heroin was basically the only kind of drug addiction then. An addict was a heroin addict. It was estimated in that era there were anywhere from 70 to 100 thousand heroin addicts in Hong Kong and one expert estimated they accounted for eighty percent of the prison population.

The methadone program didn't come into effect until 1972. It had mixed successes. The reasons why it fails in many areas are more or less the same as what happens with the Alcoholics Anonymous program. The success of any such rehabilitation program depends mostly on the individual's self discipline, determination and motivation, which are human virtues too much to ask for from an addict's fragile state of mind. The pitfall of the methadone program lies in the fickleness of the addict's behavior. The program may also backfire in that it becomes a forum for addicts to congregate, facilitating a collective relapse. It has been said that the surest way to find heroin is around the corner from a methadone clinic. Addicts are also known to get the free methadone and re-sell it for heroin money. At the clinic, they make addicts take the methadone in front of the nurse, but the addicts outsmart them by holding the drug in their mouth and spitting it out later into a bottle in the toilet. *Paak fan* is one nasty addiction.

Temple and churches

THE BIGGEST BUDDHIST TEMPLE in the area was the Chi Lin Nunnery. Chi Lin was a showcase of a temple. My family never followed the rituals or celebrated the holy days of Buddhism, but Chi Lin was an attraction for us nevertheless, because of its beautiful landscaping, pagodas, and façade. My parents would bring visitors from afar to look and walk around, and to have a few photos taken.

Among the refugee populations, especially the better-educated Shanghainese, Buddhism was considered low-brow, uncouth, and superstitious. It was prejudice, pure and simple, because the same adjectives were also applied to the Cantonese who were mostly Buddhist.

One thing I learned growing up amongst neighbors who all worshipped Buddhist gods, and among friends and classmates who were Christians, was that no one had ever tried to convert me to become a Buddhist, while there had been many attempts to convert me into a Christian.

The nuns at Chi Lin didn't try to convert me either. They pretty much kept to themselves. They stayed at the off-limit areas in the temple. And when they ventured out, they never talked to or made eye contact with anyone. My friend told me that his mom used to work in there, and some of the nuns sometimes ventured out wearing civilian clothes and wigs in disguise so that they could do things we did, such as going to a restaurant to eat meat.

Not eating meat was the nuns' big thing. All over the grounds of the nunnery, there were teachings literally carved in stone, extolling the virtues of not eating things "with a life." I still remember a catchy one, meant to deter you from eating pork, which could be translated as: "Pigs tolerate humans' bad odor, but humans praise pigs' good smell."

The nuns were a mystery to me. The fact that they were so secretive and ceremonious also inspired a powerful measure of awe in a child. But that didn't stop a brainless child from playing pranks on them. I don't mean to brag, but I might have been the only person who could get them out of their cocoon.

The temple was in a heavily wooded area, and there were lots of birds of all species flying about the trees. One day, I armed myself with a sling and a pocketful of pebbles, and decided to ambush some birds there.

What I planned to do with dead birds never entered my imbecilic mind. It just seemed like a good idea at that time.

I tried and tried, but all my shots missed the target and all the pebbles landed on the roof of the dormitory of the nuns, no doubt making a racket of the quiet life of the reclusive nuns.

An elderly nun came out and asked me why I was trying to shoot the birds. According to her, small as they were, they had heart, lungs, intestines, and liver just like us. And then she put her palms together and recited verses in what seemed to me a coded message. I presumed she was blessing the lives of living creatures, and might also be putting a curse on those who ruined them. It was a good thing I was such a lousy shot that I didn't ruin any lives. The only thing I ruined that afternoon was the tranquility of hundreds of nuns under that roof. I got an earful, but I was grateful she let me off lightly, and I never went back in there with a sling again.

Better educated and Westernized Shanghainese, if they were to follow any religion, would opt for Christianity because it was a Western religion. They usually favored a Protestant denomination instead of the Catholic church because Protestant churches were less ritualistic. My parents picked the Baptist church in the Tai Koon Yuen area, and attended the sermons there every Sunday morning, before they returned home to play mahjong in the afternoon.

I was made to go along most Sundays. The sermons were delivered in Mandarin, because most of the parishioners were better at that dialect. When there was a visiting pastor from a Western country, the sermon would be delivered in English, much to the delight of the Shanghainese, because they prided themselves in their English proficiency.

I found the preaching unconvincing. I had always thought the miracles described in the Bible were meant to be allegorical, but the preachers told the Biblical stories as if things actually happened that way. I had to restrain myself from raising my hand and contradicting the preacher at every turn. But children didn't do things like that.

The most stressful time came when they passed around the collection bag at the end of the sermon. I never had any money, and my stepmother would give me a coin or two to put into the bag. I was always tempted to put in an empty fist and save the coins for myself.

Some boy who came with his father from Tsim Sha Tsui to our church told me a joke he heard from a Western movie in which a petty thief stole from a church and when he got caught, his punch line was: "God helps those who help themselves." We thought that was the funniest thing in the world.

That boy and I tried to draw up a scheme to "help ourselves." He told me he always brought along some marbles to put in the collection bag because if you threw in marbles, you made a lot of cling-clang noises and people around would think you put in coins. On the other hand, if we used the empty-fist method, it would be silent and nobody would believe, we being snotty kids and all, that we actually put in paper money.

I promise you I never cheated with the collection bag; it was all talk and no action. It wasn't a moral decision. I was simply too much of a coward. Taking a chance with God was just not in my nature.

The Cantonese were more flexible in their religious beliefs. Tai Lin's mother worshipped all kinds of Buddhist gods, but as soon as the Catholic church around the corner from her house started giving out free food, the whole family got baptized in a hurry. Tai Lin and his two younger brothers also got their tuition fees exempted from the Catholic schools they were attending.

Even Ah Noun's family got baptized for the giveaway food. Not that it did them any good. Most times they gave the mother cheese which she thought was soap. She complained bitterly when it did not produce any lather. When finally told it was not soap but a dairy product called "Chee-see," she gave it to me because neither she nor Ah Noun could stand the smell of it. I loved cheese, and ate all that was thrown my way.

The Catholic church also gave away clothes. They were imperfect and needed some alterations or mending, and they were not fashionable. People who cared too much about "face" would decline them. One girl in the neighborhood didn't care and pranced around wearing those, but was soon nicknamed "Salvation Army."

In spite of his "Catholic" upbringing, Ah Noun was a bad boy. The church required the whole flock to go to the confession booth at least once a month. I asked Ah Noun once what he told the priest in there. He said he confessed to the same sin every time—that he had used foul language. I asked him why. He said it was extra fun to be able to repeat the foul words again and again, in front of the priest.

I went to his Catholic church often, to play table tennis. Soon they found out that I spent a lot more time at the table tennis table than in catechism classes. So they had this Mr. Lo talk to me, and basically I was told never to show my face there again.

I might have been the youngest person banned from a church in the history of Hong Kong.

A Catholic boy I went to La Salle with by the name of John Lee got wind of the situation and tried to convert me. He made me come to church and kneel in front of the altar with him, and preached to me the sermons he had received from Mr. Lo the week before. I stayed with him for as long as I could bear, hoping Mr. Lo would come by and witness the miracle. What I wouldn't do for table tennis.

I never did return to that church. I started playing soccer instead.

When I became older, I started going to the Baptist church my parents went to every Sunday, to be with the youth congregation. I spent many Saturday nights there trying to act like a responsible young adult, but secretly I was just happy to be there with the many young ladies in the congregation. The best times were around Christmas, when we had to practice choir singing night and day, so that we could spread the gospel all night long on Christmas Eve—the only night of the year we could stay out overnight with parental consent.

I couldn't sing to save my life, but the promise of female companionship made me overcome my lack of talent, inhibitions and other inadequacies. Had they known my ulterior motive, no doubt they would have kicked me out of that church, too.

Apart from the many pleasant moments singing and rubbing shoulders with members of the opposite sex, I also reaped the rewards of being seen as a churchgoer. By spending a lot of time with Christians, I was kept too busy to be led astray by Umbrella and Ah Noun.

My life then was never far from Christianity. Both Tsung Tsin and La Salle were Christian schools. La Salle took me in, even though on the application form I had proclaimed myself an atheist.

Throughout the years, I listened to a lot of sermons, and became very familiar with the Bible. Armed with that knowledge, I chose a subject called the New Testaments for the Secondary School Certificate Examination, instead of the more difficult Chinese Literature and History. I scored well on that subject, boosting my moderately successful academic record, and paving my way to Hong Kong University and a comfortable life.

In spite of what Christianity had done for me, I never became a Christian. Why? In the words of Groucho Marx, I don't care to belong to any club that will have me as a member.

Epilogue

I WAS IN MACAU on a recent visit, and went to a restaurant calling itself Wing Lai Yuen, the same name used by the restaurant at the entrance to Diamond Hill when I was a kid. A waiter showed up to take our orders. One look at him and I knew it really was the same restaurant.

I asked: "Are you. . . ?" He said yes before I finished my question. He is a member of the third generation of the same family that has run Wing Lai Yuen for decades. Yes, he has the same face as the original owner.

I ordered *dan dan* noodles. They were still the best in the world.

The restaurant received a lot of publicity when it was forced to move from Diamond Hill to Whampoa Gardens in Hung Hom a few years ago. It does very well in its new location in Hung Hom. Now, it has a branch in Macau as well.

Wing Lai Yuen was probably the last remaining icon of Diamond Hill after they chopped the area into pieces with urban development. They first built Hammer Hill Road to replace that one-lane dirt road, a continuation of Diamond Hill Road, which exited at Ngau Chi Wan. Hammer Hill Road connected uphill to Lung Cheung Road which ran all the way from east Kowloon to west Kowloon. It was the dawn of the urbanization of the whole of Kowloon.

When they built the MTR, Diamond Hill and the adjacent villages were almost totally cleared of shanty huts and old village houses, to be replaced later by high rises, except for one section of Diamond Hill Road where Wing Lai Yuen had a short lease on life and carried on business before that area was cleared as well. Then they built the Tate's Cairn Tunnel exiting in Diamond Hill. The only original thing left of the old Diamond Hill that I know of is the Chi Lin Nunnery.

I visited Chi Lin recently. It does not look like anything that I remember it to be. It is less spacious and more artificial. There is a lot more concrete and a lot less greenery than the old Chi Lin. There are no birds around for any dumb kid with a sling to terrorize. The nuns don't live there anymore, either.

Epilogue

When I was a kid in Diamond Hill, Chi Lin was a scenic attraction. Now it is a tourist attraction, with the inevitable souvenirs shop. Conservation of the Chi Lin temple has been more about renovation than preservation.

Diamond Hill is still not a precious gemstone of a place. It is now the name of an MTR station and the site of government housing estates and private housing blocks for the middle class. There is also a big shopping center complex called Hollywood Plaza, so named to commemorate the movie studios and the movie industry in Diamond Hill in the good old days. The shopping center has a glass dome roof to let in daylight. It also has a big white HOLLYWOOD sign splashed across the front using letters in the same style as used by the real thing in California.

The only remains of villages like Tai Hom and Sheung Yuen Ling are streets named after them in the neighborhood. There is a church not too far from Hollywood Plaza called Diamond Hill Baptist Church, but it is not the same one I went to. It is a new building in a new location.

The bus stops I was so familiar with are now represented by MTR stations. From Kowloon Tong eastbound, we still find familiar names such as Wong Tai Sin and Diamond Hill. There are however many new stops at new housing developments such as Lok Fu, Choi Hung, Lam Tin, and Kowloon Bay which were non-existent in my day; and Kwun Tong, which was then hard to get to and known to us as a place where salt was manufactured from sea water, is now a satellite town densely populated and full of old factories. Kowloon Tong is still a wealthy neighborhood with stand-alone houses, but is less genteel now because some of the houses have become commercial outfits, including love motels, wedding studios, and shopping centers; and one house has become the workshop of *kung fu* actor Jackie Chan.

Kowloon City hasn't changed much; most of the residential buildings are low-rise *tong lau*. It is still a big market, and jam-packed with eateries. All the stops east of Kowloon Tong still belong to the grassroots people who live in government housing or private flats in the lower price range.

The Walled City is now a park. The city underwent numerous transformations over the years. By the 60s, high rises had replaced the village houses, especially at the periphery. By the late 80s, the high rises had become so dilapidated they could make Chungking Mansions on Nathan Road look like the Four Seasons Hotel.

Epilogue

With 1997 approaching, the Hong Kong government was keen on resolving all the contentious issues of the colony before the handover. The British government, with the Chinese government's blessing, started a wholesale demolition of the city in 1990.

One of the big stories at that time was that every property owner there was compensated generously, some said too generously, since it turned out one individual actually owned more than 100 properties there.

The Walled City Park was completed in 1995, and is now a tourist attraction of historical interest. Inside the park today, there are framed scripts hung on walls, and scripts printed or engraved on murals describing historical events related to the Walled City. However, they have left out certain unsavory parts of history—there is no mention of heroin, pornography, or prostitution.

La Salle College has also changed. It is still an elite school, but the campus is not solemn and dignified anymore. Li Ka-shing struck a deal with the school board in which he built air-conditioned modern classrooms and a swimming pool for the school for free in exchange for land for him to build a row of luxurious apartments along Boundary Street.

I have kept in touch with my Diamond Hill and Tsung Tsin friends. A Cantonese saying goes like this: When we look at a person at three years old, we know what that person will be like when he or she becomes eighty years old. It's about right. My friends haven't changed at all.

Tai Lin worked as a teacher in a primary school near Kowloon City after graduating from the education college. He worked there for decades and made assistant principal until he couldn't take it anymore, and he took an early retirement a few years before the handover in 1997. He now lives in California, with his brothers and mother. He is still devoted to his two brothers, working hard in a pharmacy owned by them. He might have stopped singing love songs to his wife, but they are still happily married. He had two sons whose lives growing up were a lot better than his.

Ah Bok graduated from a Canadian university and returned to Hong Kong to work as an executive for the Hong Kong Stock Exchange. He even got rid of his Fujianese accent. He retired recently with a fat pension. He is happily married to a Shanghainese woman, and together they raised two daughters.

Chubby and Skinny didn't become lawyers or doctors.

Epilogue

Umbrella became a successful restaurateur and a multi-millionaire in London. He owned several eateries; one of which specialized in his mother's recipes. He died of cancer of the pancreas a few years ago, and made his wife a rich widow. He had been very close to his sister Joyce Wong Ting-ting, who came to visit me in 2006, a year after he died. According to her, the saddest part of his death was that his parents had to go to the funeral of their son. He bequeathed his restaurants to his only son, who, according to Joyce, is exactly like Umbrella.

Pui Chuen migrated to Vancouver in his late twenties and worked in a bank. As far as I know, he has not gambled on anything since his Diamond Hill days. He and his wife now live a quiet life in San José, California.

None of us heard from Ah Noun.

Ah Fui still lives in Kowloon City. He is one of many from Miss Yau's class I still have contact with. He studied bookkeeping and had worked for the China Light and Power Company. He is retired now. He still weighs about 100 pounds and eats five or six meals a day. He might not be interested in pornography anymore but he still gets excited over sex scandals involving the rich and famous. I am not privy to his private life, but at the start of the Aids epidemic, I got a call from him asking me all sorts of questions about how Aids could be transmitted.

Ah Yuk became a tax assessor for the Hong Kong Inland Revenue Department. He used to whisper mundane tax advice to us at the mahjong table, whether we needed it or not. He is also retired, and spends his time playing table tennis and listening to Western music. No change there.

Ah Lai studied geography in Hong Kong University and taught secondary school after graduation. He made assistant principal before retirement. When his old students met him in the street, they all forgot his real name and addressed him as Mr. Mole. Ah Lai married Ah Yuk's sister Anita Au, for a lifetime of free tax advice. They remain happily married. They have never had any vices, and have led a simple life with no luxuries and no debts. They migrated to Canada around 1997 with their two sons, and are continuing with their uneventful life there.

Cheung Ka-leung went to Canada much earlier, to study computer science, and has never been back. Like most people who act the clown, he has had a sad life. He went out with a pretty Chinese Canadian girl but after a few years the girl dumped him to marry a doctor. He ended up marrying this girl's unattractive older sister on the rebound, and it was a big mistake because the woman turned out to be a wife from hell. Among his many problems, he had to deal with his wife's spoiling one child and physically abusing the other.

Lau Lee-hok is still richer than God, but you wouldn't know it. His father didn't bequeath the family business to him right away. Instead, he made him go to Canada to study to be a doctor first, and summoned him back only after he graduated. He dresses modestly, and is not into wine, women, and song. In his spare time, he goes to the Cultural Center in Tsim Sha Tsui to watch free shows, and travels by train instead of his chauffeured Mercedes from his mansion in Yau Yat Chuen.

Ng Hon-ming has made himself a millionaire many times over by playing the Hong Kong stock market, and like any good old nouveau riche, he has become a wine connoisseur and an art collector. Although still frugal in many ways, he gives unbelievable tips to taxi drivers. He frequently says the tips his father made as a taxi driver brought him up. He gets sentimental easily, and organizes nostalgic trips back to Tsung Tsin for us. All of us became members of the Tsung Tsin Alumni Association because of him.

Lee Yat-wah became a statistician, since he knew his math. He didn't get married until a couple of years before Hong Kong's handover in 1997, when he thought it safer to migrate to another country. He married a woman with a Canadian passport. When he told us of his impending marriage, it had sounded a lot more like a business deal than a romantic journey. He is still in Canada, probably pondering over his marriage deal, now that 1997 has proven to be a non-issue.

When we last got together a few months ago, we still talked about Miss Yau. We wondered where she would be today. And in my heart I wondered where I would be today without her as my form teacher.

I spent five years in Hong Kong University studying medicine. After graduation, I interned first in Queen Mary Hospital and then in Queen Elizabeth Hospital. Soon after, I applied to go to work in the USA, because specialist training was more advanced there, and I was also fascinated by the American way of life. I joined a pathology training program at the Albert Einstein College of Medicine in New York, and after a few years of intensive training, I qualified as a "certified" pathologist. Along the way, I married an American woman from Philadelphia and together we raised three lovely children. Life in the USA was like a roller-coaster ride, but that's another story. After living there for thirteen years and a failed marriage, I returned to Hong Kong. Armed with the specialist qualification, I joined the government and soon reached the pinnacle of my career as a consultant for the Department of Health. I remarried in 1997, to a Canadian journalist. Life has been good to me.

By the time I moved back to live in Hong Kong, Diamond Hill had already had a total face-lift. No one I used to know lived there anymore. Everyone had moved on.

The unique Diamond Hill way of life made us, its one-time inhabitants, for better or worse, what we are today. We, in turn, played a part in making Hong Kong what it is today.

There is no more Diamond Hill the way it was, and there never will be again.

Long live Diamond Hill, if only in our memories, and in our hearts.

About the author

Feng Chi-shun is a naturalized US citizen, but considers Hong Kong—where he grew up and attended medical school—his home. His formative years were spent in Diamond Hill, where people were poor but life was rich.

Trained as a pathologist, he has published close to 100 scientific articles on his medical research. He was also a columnist for the *South China Morning Post*, the leading English newspaper in Hong Kong.

Feeling deprived as a child, he is making up for lost time by living life to its fullest. He is an aficionado of wine and cigars, and a part-time punter. In his spare time, he plays golf and tennis, and shoots a mean game of pool.

His three US-born children—Angel, Gina, and Stephen—and his Canadian wife Cathy are his best friends. So far, he has two grandchildren, Amirah and Qairo. He intends to live in Hong Kong for the rest of his life.

EXPLORE ASIA WITH BLACKSMITH BOOKS

From retailers around the world or from *www.blacksmithbooks.com*

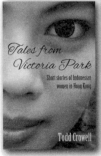